Product Innovation

and

Technology Strategy

Other Best Selling Books by the Authors

Successful Product Innovation: A Collection of Our Best
(authored by Robert G. Cooper and Scott J. Edgett)

*Winning at New Products: Accelerating the
Process from Idea to Launch,* Third Edition
(authored by Robert G. Cooper)

Lean, Rapid and Profitable New Product Development
(authored by Robert G. Cooper and Scott J. Edgett)

*Generating Breakthrough New Product Ideas:
Feeding the Innovation Funnel*
(authored by Robert G. Cooper and Scott J. Edgett)

*Product Leadership: Creating and Launching
Superior New Products,* Second Edition
(authored by Robert G. Cooper)

Portfolio Management for New Products, Second Edition
(authored by Robert G. Cooper, Scott J. Edgett
and Elko J. Kleinschmidt)

Product Development for the Service Sector
(authored by Robert G. Cooper and Scott J. Edgett)

*Best Practices in Product Innovation:
What Distinguishes Top Performers*
(authored by Robert G. Cooper, Scott J. Edgett
and Elko J. Kleinschmidt)

All books are available online at
www.stage-gate.com

Product Innovation

and

Technology Strategy

Robert G. Cooper

Scott J. Edgett

Product Development Institute Inc.

For more information on the concepts and tools introduced in this book, please visit Product Development Institute Inc. at www.prod-dev.com.

Special discounts for bulk purchases are available to corporations, academic institutions and other eligible organizations. For more information, please call +1-905-304-8798 or email info@prod-dev.com.

ISBN: 1-4392-5224-6

First Printing, August 2009

Editorial Team: Izabella Lis, Selin Dossa, Valerie Sather and Michelle Jones

Cover Design by Bonnie Katz Design
Text Design by Laura Brady

Typeset in 11 point Adobe Garamond

C O N T E N T S

CHAPTER 1

A Product Innovation
Strategy for Your Business

> I find the great thing in this world is not so much where
> we stand, as in which direction we are moving: To reach
> the port of heaven, we must sail sometimes with the
> wind and sometimes against it but we must sail, and not
> drift, and not lie at anchor.
>
> Oliver Wendell Holmes
> *The Autocrat of the Breakfast Table, 1858*

The Best Strategy Ever?

The MP3 player has been the fastest growing new consumer product ever
introduced.[1] The speed of iPod's growth has been staggering, with Apple
reaching 50 million iPods sold globally in only 4.5 years since its introduction. By contrast, it took Sony ten years to sell 50 million Walkmans.
Apple has also driven the MP3 market, whose cumulative sales reached
$200 million by the end of 2006, of which Apple was responsible for one
quarter (and hit a 70 percent market share in the US). Compare that
market growth to wireless phones, which took 12 years to reach sales of
50 million, or digital cameras, or cell phones which had much slower
starts. In the last quarter of 2008, 22 million iPods were sold, representing
42 percent of Apple's revenue. The growth continues.[2]

So how did Apple pull off this amazing coup? Contrary to popular
belief, Apple *was not the innovator* in this industry – it did not invent the

portable MP3 player. Indeed, when the iPod was introduced in November of 2001, there were more than 50 companies selling portable MP3 players in the US; many were Asian companies relying on the Internet to market their products.

Apple's success where others failed was due to a brilliantly conceived innovation strategy that was superbly executed. In broadest terms, Apple saw the growing market need, and then identified and solved the major problems with existing MP3 players: size, storage capacity, user interface, and the shortage of legally downloadable music. In solving the problems, Apple leveraged its unique strengths perfectly: Its ability to vertically integrate and deliver an "amalgam of hardware, software and content that made buying, storing and playing music virtually effortless. Apple achieved this by relying on its legendary expertise in hardware and software but without going into the music business".[3] Apple also positioned the iPod cleverly, targeting its loyal customer base of young, media- and tech-savvy people (Apple's original target market) with a product that almost became a fashion statement. Apple used its effective system of distribution channels, maintained its high-quality image and avoided price discounting.

Sony, which had dominated the portable music market since the introduction of the Walkman in 1979, possessed many strengths and competencies as well: size, brand name and image, distribution and market presence, technology, and manufacturing capabilities. But it selected a strategy that missed the boat. As if Sony had not learned anything from its failed Betamax strategy, instead of attacking the embryonic but growing MP3 market, it rejected the opportunity. Instead Sony tried to defend its languishing digital mini-disc player and establish it as the next device to supplant the declining CD player, the Discman. The rest is history.

Apple's successful iPod "imitation strategy" has had a huge impact on the company's fortunes. Its revenue more than tripled from 2001 to 2006, while the income statement went from a $20 million loss in profits to plus $2 billion… another case of brilliant innovation strategy, flawlessly executed (to Sony's chagrin, whose case of a poorly conceived strategy was doomed to failure). Brilliant strategy rules again!

Win the Battle, But Lose the War?

Unlike Apple, but like its rivals, most companies lack an effective innovation strategy. Ask any senior executive what their company's innovation strategy is and you'll most likely get one of three responses:

1. A blank stare or look of bewilderment, like "what's this guy talking about?",
2. An outline of their business plan, which is really a financial plan that says little about direction for product innovation,
3. A list of this year's major product development initiatives.

All three responses indicate a failure to comprehend what an innovation strategy is or does. An innovation strategy is not a financial plan, and it is not a business strategy (although the business strategy and innovation strategy are closely linked, and in some businesses, the innovation strategy is embedded within the business strategy). A list of active development projects is not an innovation strategy either – these are the tactics and deal with the short term, often the manifestation of the strategy, but not the strategy per se. So if these or similar responses describe your business, then keep reading!

Tactics and Strategy: What If . . .

- What if your business had implemented a world-class idea-to-launch system – a process to guide development projects from idea-to-market?
- What if you had a superb portfolio management system to help select projects – to help your executives make the right new product development investment decisions?
- And what if you had created a very positive climate and culture for innovation within your business, with senior management strongly supporting innovation at every opportunity?

Would the result be a high performing business in terms of new products? Not necessarily. One of the most important drivers of success in product innovation is missing: One of the four points of performance of the *Innovation Diamond*™, namely your innovation strategy (Exhibit 1.1). And that driver makes the difference between winning individual new product battles and winning the entire product innovation war.[4,5]

Your business's product innovation strategy charts the strategy for your business's entire new product effort. It is the master plan: It provides the direction for your enterprise's new product developments, and it is the essential link between your product development effort and your total business strategy.[6]

The Innovation Diamond

Our major benchmarking research on high performing businesses reveals that there are *four major drivers* of performance. We refer to them as the Innovation Diamond.[7] These four points of best practice stand out as common denominators among the top performing businesses. The four points of the Innovation Diamond are:

1. *Product Innovation and Technology Strategy:* Top performers put a product innovation and technology strategy in place, driven by the leadership team and the strategic vision of the business. This product innovation strategy provides focus, guides the business's product development direction, and steers resource allocation, investment decisions and project selection. They have a strategic focus.

2. *Resource Commitment and Portfolio Management:* Top performers commit sufficient resources to their total product innovation effort and to individual initiatives. Further, they boast an effective portfolio management system that helps the leadership team allocate these resources to the right areas and to the right development projects.[8]

3. *Idea-to-Launch System – Stage-Gate®:* The Stage-Gate system exists in top performing businesses, which drives new product projects from the idea phase through to launch and beyond.[9] This idea-to-launch system

emphasizes feeding the innovation funnel with robust ideas, solid front-end homework on development projects (including voice-of-customer input), tough Go/Kill decision points from end to end, and quality of execution throughout. At the same time, the system in top performers is agile, flexible, scalable and adaptable.[10]

4. *Climate, Culture, Teams and Leadership:* Senior managers in top performing businesses create a positive climate and culture for innovation and entrepreneurship, foster effective cross-functional new product project teams, and are themselves properly engaged in the product development decision making process. They create the right environment for innovation.

These are the principal practices that separate the best performers in product innovation from the rest, as identified in our research. Procter & Gamble (P&G) is one company that has implemented their version of the Innovation Diamond.[11] Consider a success story within P&G that illustrates how these points of performance impact on business results.

EXHIBIT 1.1: The Innovation Diamond shows the four drivers of performance in product innovation – the common denominators of top performing firms.

The Cosmetics Business Story at P&G

Procter & Gamble's cosmetics business is a case in point where a dramatic turnaround was achieved via a disciplined, holistic and strategic approach to new product management. The story took shape when P&G acquired *Oil of Olay*, a skin cream as part of the Richardson-Vicks purchase in 1985, and then the *Cover Girl* and *Clarion* cosmetics brands in 1989. Two years later *Max Factor* was acquired.

P&G then applied its tried-and-true approach of leveraging scale and a new product strategy consisting of a few, big new products. But there was no effective innovation strategy: Efforts were scattered and unfocused as the business tried to do everything in many different product categories and segments. So, by 1994, management was forced to retreat and retrench. P&G dropped the Clarion line, and through much of the 1990s, senior management at P&G wondered if they should be in the cosmetic business at all. A new cosmetics line under the *Oil of Olay* banner was attempted; but the new line failed, and the entire cosmetics business continued to decline.

The business turnaround started in the late 1990s, when management turned to their *Initiatives Diamond* (shown in Exhibit 1.2).[12] The first element of P&G's Diamond is a product innovation strategy. Indeed, the real breakthrough occurred when the leadership team began a rigorous strategic planning process leading to clearly defined goals, objectives, strategies and measures. A much more concentrated innovation strategy was selected which focused on lips, face and eyes, rather than rest of the body. A second facet of strategy focused on getting the supply chain under control by applying end-to-end supply chain management. The supply chain was streamlined so that production and shipments were tied to market demand. As a result, time in the supply chain was reduced, thereby eliminating much of the product obsolescence generated with each new product launch.

Next, management applied the second element of P&G's Initiatives Diamond: their SIMPL new product Stage-Gate process. SIMPL is a methodology for driving new product projects from the idea phase through

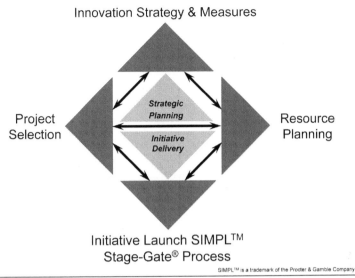

Innovation Strategy & Measures

Project
Selection

Strategic
Planning

Initiative
Delivery

Resource
Planning

Initiative Launch SIMPL™
Stage-Gate® Process

SIMPL™ is a trademark of the Procter & Gamble Company

EXHIBIT 1.2: Procter & Gamble Company's Initiatives Diamond serves as a guide to each business's new product efforts.

to launch, and incorporates many P&G best practices. It is a rigorous product launch process using stage-and-gate decision making, complete with clear Go/Kill criteria and timing requirements. One resulting big success is *Outlast* by *Cover Girl* (a kiss-proof, long-lasting lipstick that uses a unique two-part application system, first a color and then a gloss, to produce an enduring lip color). A second winner – *Lipfinity* by *Max Factor* – was also introduced, again using the SIMPL idea-to-launch system. And the *Oil of Olay* line has been leveraged successfully, again using the focused innovation strategy, this time concentrating on facial lines that come with aging. *Oil of Olay's Regenerist* has been a huge success, which has taken this tired brand from sales of $200 million in 1985 to $2 billion today.[13]

Portfolio management, a third element of P&G's Initiatives Diamond, was employed to enable management to look at the entire portfolio of new product initiatives to achieve the right balance and mix. Through portfolio management, the business built a pipeline of new and improved products that established the needed initiative rhythm for each product line (face, lips, eyes) – new products and upgrades timed to create news and excitement in the market. This "launch and sustain" portfolio approach was a key part of winning in the marketplace.

Today, P&G's cosmetics business is a healthy, growing, and profitable enterprise. Performance results have significantly improved since the late 1990s, and the business is seen as a key growth engine for P&G. But the turnaround did not happen by chance. One key to success was getting new products right – the development of an integrated business and product innovation strategy, coupled with an effective idea-to-launch process (SIMPL) and first-rate portfolio management to ensure a steady stream of the right kinds of new and improved products.

Are Innovation Diamond Drivers Missing In Your Business?

How does your business fare on these drivers in the Innovation Diamond? Many companies have implemented idea-to-launch processes (an estimated 73 percent of product developers in the US now employ a stage-and-gate system); and our research reveals that most companies understand the need for fostering the right climate and culture for innovation. Similarly, portfolio management – making the right project investment decisions – is a hot topic among leading product development companies, although our research reveals that many have yet to figure out how to do portfolio management properly. But the weakest link, and the vital missing success driver, is the *product innovation and technology strategy* shown in Exhibit 1.1.

Consider the facts in Exhibit 1.3. Here you see what percentage of businesses we studied that had each of the key elements of a product innovation strategy in place for their business:[14]

- Just over one-third have clearly defined and articulated new product objectives for the business – which means that almost two-thirds of firms do not!
- Less than half of businesses define the role that new products will play in achieving their overall business goals. Defining their product

innovation objectives, and what role innovation would play in achieving the business goals, was the kick-start to success in P&G's cosmetic business.

- Just over one-third have a long-term commitment to and strategy for product innovation. The great majority have short-term and tactical outlooks, for example, strategy boils down to a list of active projects in their development pipeline.

- The majority of businesses define areas of strategic focus for their innovation efforts, but many executives expressed concern that these areas of focus were poorly chosen and perhaps were the wrong areas (much like Sony's poor choices in the MP3 example).

- Only one-quarter of businesses translate strategy into reality by making vital spending decisions. For example, few companies use the powerful technique of strategic buckets to ensure the right balance and mix of development initiatives. Strategic product

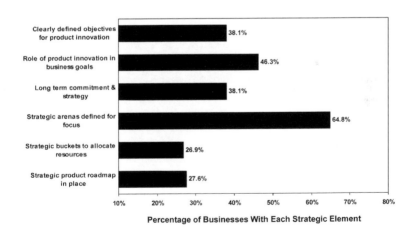

Percentage of Businesses With Each Strategic Element

EXHIBIT 1.3: These are the key elements of a Product Innovation Strategy, and they are missing in most businesses.

roadmapping, a method that earmarks resources for major development initiatives over five-to-seven years, is missing in the majority of firms.

The next section begins with a definition of what the word "strategy" means. We then look at the hard evidence in support of strategy – facts that make it imperative that you and your leadership team develop a product innovation strategy for your business. We show how some types of strategies are closely linked to business performance. Next, the elements or components of an innovation strategy are defined, followed by a glimpse into some of the broad strategic options that your business might choose in product innovation. So let's move forward and play the role of the General, looking at strategy and direction for the business's entire new product effort. Let's go win the innovation war!

What is a Product Innovation Strategy?

The Meaning of "Strategy"

Many people use the word "strategy" incorrectly, because they don't understand what the word means and what a good strategy is. Broadly speaking, a product innovation strategy is a master plan that guides your business's new product efforts. But how does one specifically define or describe a product innovation strategy?

The term "strategy" is derived from the Greek word *stratēgos*, which in turn is derived from two words: *stratos* (army) and *ago* (ancient Greek for "leading"). *Stratēgos* referred to a "military commander" during the age of Athenian democracy. Not surprisingly, much of history's development and writing on strategy is from military sources. For example, classic texts such as Sun Tzu's *The Art of War* written in China 2,500 years ago, the political strategy of Niccolo Machiavelli's *The Prince* written in 1513, or Carl von Clausewitz's *On War* published in 1832 are still well-known and highly influential in military circles today.

In the last half of the twentieth century, the concept of strategic management was applied to organizations, typically to business firms and corporations. Thus, as business managers and executives, we are relative novices when it comes to strategy and strategic concepts; so it is little wonder that most of us struggle a bit. Nonetheless, many of our principles of business strategy are derived from the development and practice of military strategy over the centuries. For example, from the *United States Army Field Manual,* here are some strategic principles:[15]

- *Objective*: Direct every military operation toward a clearly defined, decisive and attainable objective
- *Offensive*: Seize, retain and exploit the initiative
- *Mass*: Concentrate combat power at the decisive place and time
- *Economy of force*: Allocate minimum essential combat power to secondary efforts
- *Unity of command*: For every objective, ensure unity of effort under one responsible commander
- *Simplicity*: Prepare clear, uncomplicated plans and clear, concise orders to ensure thorough understanding.

Some of these principles sound uncannily familiar to business strategists, and they should as our strategy theories and principles are largely based on military principles. The field of product innovation strategy, or the company's "offensive strategy", has particularly close links to military strategy. For example, the need for focus and for defining strategic arenas is based on the principle of "mass", noted above; our "strategic buckets" concept is about deployment of resources to arenas; "roadmapping", a popular concept today in business, comes from the General's view of how to achieve the objective. Even the term "strategic arena" has a military connection. So on occasion, we use military analogies and terms, not because we are war-like, but simply because of the history and derivation of modern strategic concepts in businesses today.

In a business context, strategy has been defined as "the schemes whereby a firm's resources and advantages are managed (deployed) in order to surprise and surpass competitors or to exploit opportunities".[16] Strategic change is defined as "a realignment of a firm's product-market environment".[17] Strategy is closely tied to product and market specification. That is, strategy is about choosing the markets to target and choosing the products to target them with.[18]

In this book, "business strategy" refers to the business's overall strategy. Product innovation strategy is a component of, or flows from, that business strategy, and deals specifically with new products and new services.[19] And by product innovation strategy, we do not mean a vaguely worded statement of intent, one that approaches a vision or mission statement. We mean operational, action-specific strategies that include defined objectives, arenas of strategic focus, deployment decisions, and attack and entry plans. If these principles are good enough for our Generals, they are good enough for us.

What Strategy Looks Like

The Innovation Diamond in Exhibit 1.1 shows the important drivers of product innovation performance, but it does not show all the pieces necessary to make innovation happen in your business. And sometimes it gets confusing when one tries to fit the pieces together. We are often asked, "What's the difference between portfolio management and pipeline management?" or "How does project management fit in?" Exhibit 1.4 does a comprehensive job of outlining just where the pieces all fit, and it also provides brief definitions of each of these pieces.

It all begins with your business strategy (top of Exhibit 1.4) which defines the overall direction of the organization. This strategy drives the product innovation and technology strategy which, in turn, drives portfolio management. Portfolio management operationalizes the innovation strategy by making spending decisions (for example, strategic buckets and strategic product roadmaps). Next, pipeline management, which is tactical rather than strategic, prioritizes projects and makes resource allocations to specific projects. The new product idea-to-launch process (stage-and-gate system) guides, directs and accelerates individual projects,

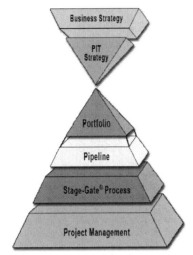

Business Strategy – Defines the overall strategic direction of the organization

Product Innovation & Technology Strategy – Defines objectives and identifies the strategic arenas for innovation for the business

Portfolio - Operationalizes the product innovation and technology strategy (e.g. Strategic Buckets)

Pipeline - Prioritizes projects to tactically allocate resources

Stage-Gate Process – Guides, directs and accelerates the innovation efforts from idea through launch

Project Management – Manages the budgets and milestones of individual projects

EXHIBIT 1.4: From strategy (top), all else flows. The Product Innovation Strategy flows from, or is part of, the Business Strategy for the organization and it, in turn, drives the Portfolio (project selection) and development pipeline.

kills bad projects, and drives good ones forward. Finally, project management, the most tactical of all systems in Exhibit 1.4, manages the budgets and milestones of individual projects.

Why Have a Product Innovation Strategy At All?

Developing a product innovation strategy is hard work. It involves many people, especially top management. Why go to all the effort? Most of us can probably name countless companies that do not appear to have a master plan for their new product effort. How do they get by?

Running an innovation program without a strategy is like running a war without a military strategy. There's no direction, and the results are often highly unsatisfactory. On occasion, unplanned efforts do succeed, but it is largely owing to good luck or, perhaps, brilliantly-executed tactics.

A new product effort without a strategy will inevitably lead to a number of ad hoc decisions made independently of one another. New product and research and development (R&D) projects are often initiated solely on their individual merits with little regard to their fit into the grander scheme. Portfolio management is all but impossible, for example. The result is that the business finds itself in unrelated or unwanted markets, products, and technologies. In other words, there is no focus; it is a scattergun effort (much like P&G's first years in the cosmetics business).

Objectives and Role – The Necessary Link to Your Overall Business Strategy

What type of direction does a product innovation strategy give a business's new product efforts? First, the objectives of your product innovation strategy tie your product development effort tightly to your overall business strategy. New product development, so often viewed in a "hands-off" fashion by senior management, becomes a central part of the business strategy, a key plank in the overall strategic platform.

The question of spending commitments on new products is dealt with by defining the role and objectives of the new product effort. Too often the R&D or new product budget is easy prey in hard economic times.

Spending on development and new product marketing tends to be viewed as discretionary expenditures, something that can be slashed if need be. However, if you establish product innovation as a central facet of your business's overall strategy, and if you firmly define the role and objectives of product innovation, cutting the R&D budget becomes much less arbitrary. Consequently, there is a continuity of resource commitment to new products.

The Strategic Arenas – Guiding the War Effort

A second facet of the product innovation strategy, the definition of arenas, is critical to guiding and focusing your new product efforts. The first step in your idea-to-launch new product process is idea generation. But where does one search for new product ideas? Unless the arenas are defined, the idea search is undirected, unfocused, and ineffective.

Your business's product innovation strategy is also fundamental to project selection and portfolio management. Strategy drives the entire project selection process. Without a definition of your playing fields – the arenas of strategic focus – good luck in trying to make effective project screening decisions.

The definition of arenas also guides long-term resource and personnel planning. If certain markets are designated as top priority, then the business can acquire resources, people, skills, and knowledge to enable it to attack those markets. Similarly, if certain technologies are singled out as arenas, the business can hire and acquire resources and technologies to bolster its abilities in those fields, or perhaps even seek alliances with other firms. Resource building doesn't happen overnight. One can't buy a sales force on a moment's notice, and one can't acquire a critical mass of key researchers or engineers in a certain technology at the local supermarket. Putting the right people, resources, and skills in place takes both lead time and direction.

The Evidence in Support of Strategy

The argument in favor of a product innovation strategy, although logical, may be somewhat theoretical. One can't help but think of all those companies that have made it without a grand strategy. Further, the notion of deciding what's in versus what's out of bounds is foreign to many businesses.[20]

So where is the evidence to support having a product innovation strategy? The studies that have looked at businesses' new product strategies have a clear and consistent message: A product innovation strategy at the business unit or company level is critical to ongoing and continual success, and some strategies clearly work better than others. Consider these facts:

1. Ten best management practices were identified in a study of 79 leading R&D organizations.[21] Near the top of the list is "use a formal development process", an endorsement of the use of stage-and-gate processes. Even higher on the list is "coordinate long-range business planning and R&D plans" – a call for a new product or R&D plan for the business that meshes with the business plan. Although adoption of these best practices varies widely by company, the study revealed that high performers tend to embrace these best practices more than do low performers.

2. Booz, Allen & Hamilton's study of new product practices found that businesses most likely to succeed in the development and launch of new products are those that implement a company-specific approach, driven by business objectives and strategies, with a *well-defined product innovation strategy* at its core – see Exhibit 1.5. The product innovation strategy was viewed as instrumental to the effective identification of market and product opportunities.[22] The authors of this study explain why having a product innovation strategy is tied to success:

> "A product innovation strategy links the new product process to company objectives, and provides focus for idea or concept generation and for establishing appropriate screening criteria. The outcome of this strategy analysis is a set of strategic roles, used not to generate specific new product ideas, but to help identify markets for which new products will be developed. These market opportunities provide the set of product and market requirements from which new product ideas are generated. In addition, strategic roles provide guidelines for new product performance measurement criteria. Performance thresholds tied to strategic roles provide a more precise means of screening new product ideas."

Businesses that are most likely to succeed at new products are those:[1]
- that implement a company-specific new product idea-to-launch process
- are driven by business objectives and strategies
- with a well-defined *new product strategy* at its core

Our benchmarking studies reveal that:[2]
- having an articulated new product strategy for the business is one of the *four most important drivers* of new product performance

The need for an articulated product innovation strategy is clear
How well-defined is the innovation strategy for your business?

1 Source: Booz-Allen & Hamilton
2 Source: APQC Cooper, Edgett & Kleinschmidt benchmarking study

EXHIBIT 1.5: Having a product innovation strategy for your business is vital to success, according to several major studies of innovation results.

3. In a major benchmarking study we found that having an articulated product innovation strategy is one of the four important drivers of new product performance (the Innovation Diamond in Exhibit 1.1).[23] Top performing businesses in product innovation have a defined product innovation strategy. Such a strategy specifies objectives and the role of new products. It defines arenas of strategic focus and thrust (and their priorities), it outlines a product roadmap and has a longer term orientation. Look at the results in Exhibit 1.6: Top performers have these strategic elements in place much more so than do poor performers. As a result, these businesses achieve better new product results. They are better able to meet their new product sales and profit objectives; their new product effort has a much greater positive impact on the business; and, they achieve higher success rates at launch.

4. The performance impact of product innovation strategies in 120 businesses was investigated in one of our own studies that probed deeply firms' product innovation strategies.[24] This study is the first

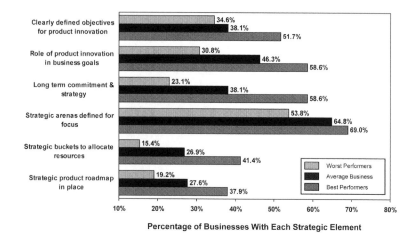

Strategic Element	Worst Performers	Average Business	Best Performers
Clearly defined objectives for product innovation	34.6%	38.1%	51.7%
Role of product innovation in business goals	30.8%	46.3%	58.6%
Long term commitment & strategy	23.1%	38.1%	58.6%
Strategic arenas defined for focus	53.8%	64.8%	69.0%
Strategic buckets to allocate resources	15.4%	26.9%	41.4%
Strategic product roadmap in place	19.2%	27.6%	37.9%

Percentage of Businesses With Each Strategic Element

EXHIBIT 1.6: Top performing businesses have a Product Innovation and Technology Strategy complete with these key elements above; poor performers do not.

published investigation undertaken on a large number of businesses that considers many strategy dimensions, and how the strategy of the business's new product effort is tied to performance results. The overriding conclusion is that product innovation strategy and performance are strongly linked. The types of markets, products and technologies that firms elect, and the orientation and direction of their product innovation efforts, have a pronounced impact on success and profitability. Strategy really does count!

Four strategic thrusts, or themes, were identified as common denominators among businesses that outperform the rest in product innovation (Exhibit 1.7):

1. Focused on one or a few key areas (as opposed to scattergun)
2. Strong technology and technologically driven
3. Strongly market focused, with solid market inputs
4. Offensive (as opposed to defensive).

1. **A focused new product effort is more successful**
   - Developing new products that are focused on one or a few areas (markets, sectors, applications)
   - Developing new products that are closely related (linked) to each other
   - Opposite of a highly diverse or scatter-gun approach
2. **Technologically driven strategies do better**
   - Having strong technology and technological prowess
   - Employing sophisticated development technologies
   - Developing high-technology, technically complex new products
3. **Market-focused strategies do better**
   - Proactive in market-need identification
   - Highly sensitive to market needs and wants, solid market inputs and insights
   - Products are developed closely in tune with market wants
4. **An offensive orientation outperforms a defensive stance**
   - Viewing their new product initiatives as aggressive ones
   - Aimed at growth and gaining market share (rather than merely protecting a position)

EXHIBIT 1.7: Four strategic thrusts or themes lead to better product innovation performance.

These four "winning thrusts" or themes make sense; they are certainly feasible, as witnessed by the significant minority of firms that had adopted them successfully; and they are not mutually exclusive (that is, a business can adopt two or three of these themes at the same time). Based on the four themes uncovered in this study, we identified three innovation strategy types. Each is explained here and illustrated in Exhibits 1.8-1.10:

- *Type A:* The strategy that yields best performance results is labeled the *Differentiated Strategy* in Exhibit 1.8. It is a technologically sophisticated and aggressive effort, very focused, with a strong market orientation. In this strategy, the business targets attractive high-growth, high-potential markets with premium-priced, strongly differentiated, superior and high-quality products. This strategy leads to the highest percentage of sales by new products (47 percent versus 35 percent for the other businesses); the highest success rates at launch; higher profitability levels; and greater new product impact on the business's sales and profits.

Type A – The Differentiated Strategy (15.6% of businesses)

- A technologically sophisticated and driven one
- A high degree of product fit and focus
- A strong market focus
- Targets attractive high-growth, high-potential markets where competition is weaker
- New products – premium-priced, strong differentiation
- High-quality products that meet customer needs better
- Products that offer unique benefits to the customer

Leads to the best results:

- The highest percentage of sales by new products
- The highest success rates at launch
- A higher profitability level
- Greater new product impact on the business's sales and profits

EXHIBIT 1.8: Strategy Type A yields the best results in product innovation, but represents only 15 percent of businesses.

- *Type B:* The next best strategy is the *Low-Budget Conservative Strategy* outlined in Exhibit 1.9. It is characterized by low relative R&D spending and features me-too, undifferentiated new products; but it has a highly focused and a "stay-close-to-home" approach. New products match the business's production and technological skills and resources, fitting into the business's existing product lines, and are aimed at familiar and existing markets. This type of strategy achieves respectable results. The business's new product effort is profitable relative to spending, but yields a low proportion of sales by new products and has a low impact on the business's sales and profits. This conservative strategy results in an efficient, safe, and profitable new product effort, but one lacking a dramatic impact on the business.

- *Type C:* This is the most popular strategy. It is the one employed consciously or unconsciously by more of the businesses and is displayed in Exhibit 1.10 as *The Technology Push Strategy.* These businesses have a technologically sophisticated and innovative new product effort, are strongly R&D oriented, and are proactive in

Type B – The Low-Budget Conservative Strategy
(23.8% of businesses)
- Low R&D spending
- Develop copy-cat, me too, undifferentiated new products
- Efforts are focused
- Highly synergistic with the base business
- A 'stay-close-to-home' approach

They achieve moderately positive results:
- A high proportion of successes; low failure and kill rates
- Profitable
- Yields a low proportion of sales by new products and has a low impact on the business's sales and profits

This conservative strategy results in an efficient, safe and profitable new product effort
- But one lacking a dramatic impact on the business

EXHIBIT 1.9: Strategy Type B is much more conservative, and yields good results, but not as good as Type A.

acquiring new development technologies and generating new product ideas. The innovation effort is strongly offensive (versus defensive) and viewed as a leading edge of the business's overall strategy. The new products developed here are innovative, high-technology, technically complex, and often the result of high-risk and venturesome projects. But these businesses totally lack a market orientation: The development process is dominated by the technical community, and customer input is noticeable by its absence. Consequently, poor markets are chosen – low potential, small size, low growth and minimal need. And, the projects tend to be "step-out", far removed from the company's existing product lines, internal strengths and competencies. The results are predicable; costly, inefficient innovation projects plagued by high failure rates.

We identified two more strategies which yield even worse results. The point is that there is a strong connection between the product innovation strategy (whether that strategy is elected by design or by accident) and the

Type C – The Technology Push Strategy (26.2% of businesses)

- The most popular strategy
- A technologically driven approach to product innovation
- Firms are technologically sophisticated, technology oriented & innovative
- New product effort lacks a strong market focus and market inputs
- Little fit, synergy or focus in the types of products and markets – scattergun

Leads to mediocre performance results:

- Fails to meet the business's new product objectives
- Yields a high proportion of project cancellations and failures
- Less profitable than Type A or B above

Technology Push strategy produces a technologically aggressive, moderately high-impact effort...

- But is costly, inefficient and plagued by failures
- Because of:
    - A lack of focus
    - A lack of marketing orientation & input

EXHIBIT 1.10: Strategy Type C is the most popular strategy, but yields inferior results compared to Types A or B.

performance results it achieves. Obviously, conceiving and pursing a deliberate innovation strategy, perhaps similar to Type A or B above, is certain to yield better results. We recommend incorporating some of the key thrusts we identified: For example, keeping the strategy technologically driven combined with a strong market focus, concentrating on a few key areas and taking an offensive (as opposed to defensive) approach.

Convinced yet? Yes, there are always a few outlier firms that defy the rule and get lucky now and then without much of a strategy for innovation. But if sustained, consistent and long-term performance is the goal, then all the evidence points to the need for a clearly defined, carefully crafted innovation strategy for the business as one of the keys to success.

The Elements of a Product Innovation Strategy and Their Impacts

Six elements of a product innovation strategy strongly distinguish the top performing businesses in product innovation (Exhibit 1.6). These strategy elements also provide insights into how to go about developing a product innovation strategy for your business. They are the basis for the ideal logical flow or "thought process" to guide your leadership team in developing an insightful product innovation strategy (Exhibit 1.11). So let's look at each of these elements, what they are and why they are so critical:

1. Objectives and Role: Begin with your goals! The business's product innovation strategy specifies the objectives of the new product effort, and it indicates the role that product innovation will play in helping the company achieve its business objectives. It answers the question: How do new products and product innovation fit into our business's overall plan? A statement such as "By the year 2012, 30 percent of our business's sales will come from new products" is a typical objective. Sub-objectives can also be stated, such as the desired number of major new product introductions, expected success rates, and desired financial returns from new products.

This ingredient of strategy – having clear objectives – would seem fairly basic. What is surprising is how many businesses lack clear, written objectives for their overall new product efforts. Note the mediocre scores in Exhibit 1.6: On average, only 38.1 percent of businesses proficiently define such product innovation objectives. By contrast, the majority (51.7 percent) of best performers do spell out their new product objectives; and, the worst performers are quite weak here with only 34.6 percent defining objectives. Having clearly articulated product innovation objectives for your business is, thus, a mandatory best practice.

Another key best practice is to ensure that the role of new products in achieving the business's goals is clear and communicated to all (also highlighted in Exhibit 1.6). The whole point of having goals is so that everyone involved in the activity has a common purpose, something to work toward. Yet, far too often, personnel who work on new product projects are not aware of their business's new product objectives, or the role that new products will play in achieving the total business objectives. What we witness here are very mediocre practices: Only 46.3 percent of businesses define and communicate the role of product innovation in realizing their business goals. However, 58.6 percent of best performers do define this role (versus only 30.8 percent of the worst performers), and this element of an innovation strategy is the most strongly correlated with new product performance. It is clearly a best practice. (More on defining innovation objectives in the next chapter).

2. *Arenas and Strategic Thrust:* Focus is the key to an effective product innovation strategy. Your product innovation strategy specifies where you'll attack or, perhaps more importantly, where you won't attack. Thus the concept of *strategic arenas* is at the heart of a new product strategy – the markets, industry sectors, applications, product types or technologies on which your business will focus its new product efforts, as shown in the top part of Exhibit 1.11. This is similar to the *principle of mass* in military strategy; the resources must be concentrated at a decisive place and time. The key battlefields must be defined!

Here, businesses on average do a solid job, with 64.8 percent identifying and designating strategic arenas in order to help focus their product development efforts (Exhibit 1.6). Best performers define strategic arenas more so than do worst performers: 69.0 percent versus 53.8 percent; and, this strategy element is again strongly correlated with performance.

The specification of these arenas – what is "in bounds" and what is "out of bounds" – is fundamental to spelling out the direction or strategic thrust of the business's product development effort. It is the result of identifying and assessing product innovation opportunities at the strategic level. Without arenas defined, the search for specific new product ideas or opportunities is unfocused. Over time, the portfolio of new product projects is likely to contain a lot of unrelated projects, in many different

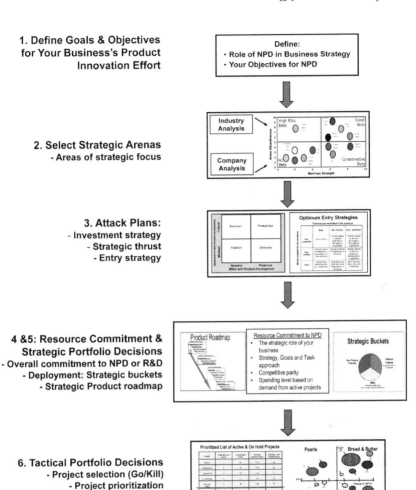

1. Define Goals & Objectives for Your Business's Product Innovation Effort

2. Select Strategic Arenas
- Areas of strategic focus

3. Attack Plans:
- Investment strategy
- Strategic thrust
- Entry strategy

4 &5: Resource Commitment & Strategic Portfolio Decisions
- Overall commitment to NPD or R&D
- Deployment: Strategic buckets
- Strategic Product roadmap

6. Tactical Portfolio Decisions
- Project selection (Go/Kill)
- Project prioritization
- Resource commitments to projects

EXHIBIT 1.11: The first major steps in crafting a Product Innovation Strategy for your business includes defining objectives, selecting strategic arenas, and developing attack plans. After the strategic arenas are selected and the general attack plans are decided, the critical spending and deployment decisions must be made. Tactics (not part of strategy) logically flow next.

markets, technologies or product-types – a scatter-gun effort. The results are predicable – a not-so-profitable new product effort.

> *Example:* One DuPont polymers business faced exactly this problem; much money spent on R&D, but no focus because there was no strategy or defined arenas. Senior management recognized the deficiency. Management first identified a number of possible arenas (product-market-technology areas) which might be "in bounds". They assessed each in terms of their market attractiveness and the opportunity for leveraging the business's core competencies. They then selected several arenas and began to focus their new product initiatives within these chosen arenas.

(More on the definition and selection of arenas in Chapters 3 and 4.)

3. Attack Strategy and Entry Strategy: The issue of how to attack each strategic arena should also be part of your product innovation strategy (Exhibit 1.11). For example, the strategy may be to be quite aggressive and be the industry innovator, the first to the market with new products; or, the attack strategy may be to be a "fast follower", waiting and watching, and rapidly copying and improving upon competitive entries. Other strategies focus on being low cost versus a differentiator versus a niche player. The global dimension is part of the attack plan: whether to adopt a global, "glocal" or regional strategic approach to product development. Additionally, when planning to enter a new arena, entry strategies must be crafted. They can include internal product development, licensing, joint venturing, partnering, alliances and even acquisitions of other firms (more on attack plans in Chapter 5).

4. Deployment – Spending Commitments, Priorities and Strategic Buckets: Strategy becomes real when you start spending money! So, your product innovation strategy must deal with deployment of resources – with how much to spend on product innovation; and it should indicate the relative emphasis, or strategic priorities, accorded each strategic arena where you will focus your efforts (Exhibit 1.11). Thus, an important facet of a product innovation strategy is resource commitment and allocation. The ear-marking buckets of resources (funds or person-days targeted at different strategic arenas or project types) helps to ensure the strategic alignment of product innovation with your overall business goals.[25]

Many best-in-class companies use the concept of strategic buckets to help in this deployment decision. But the use of strategic buckets is a decidedly weak area overall with only 26.9 percent of businesses doing this well. The use of strategic buckets is clearly a best practice, with 41.4 percent of best performers employing this strategic buckets approach and only 15.4 of worst performers. (More on how to develop strategic buckets in Chapter 5).

5. The Strategic Product Roadmap – Major Initiatives and Platform Developments: A strategic roadmap is an effective way to map out a series of major initiatives in an attack plan. A roadmap is simply a management group's view of how to get where they want to go or to achieve their desired objective.[26]

Your product innovation strategy should, therefore, map out the planned assaults – your major new product initiatives and their timing – that are required in order to succeed in a certain market or sector. This should be in the form of a *strategic product roadmap*[1]. This roadmap may also specify the platform developments required for these new products. Additionally, the development or acquisition of new technologies may be laid out in the form of a technology roadmap.

The use of roadmaps is a weak area generally, with only 27.6 percent of businesses developing product roadmaps proficiently. About twice as many best performers (37.9 percent) use product roadmaps than do worst performers (19.2 percent). (Roadmaps are the topic of Chapter 6.)

---

[1] The term "product roadmap" has come to have many meanings in business. Here we mean a *strategic* roadmap, which lays out the major initiatives and platforms envisioned into the future – as opposed to a tactical roadmap, which lists each and every product, extension, modification, tweak, etc.

Once these five strategy steps are complete, management can then deal with the next level of decision making: Translating strategy into reality; namely making the tactical decisions (bottom of Exhibit 1.11).[27]

6. Tactical: Individual Project Selection: Tactical decisions focus on individual projects, but obviously follow from the strategic decisions. Questions typically addressed are: What specific new product projects should you undertake? What resources should be allocated to each? What are their relative priorities? Even when a product roadmap has been sketched out strategically (above), it tends to be conceptual and directional; one still must look at each and every project and decide whether or not it is really a Go. And while resource spending splits (also known as buckets) are useful directional guides, Go decisions on specific projects must still be made. (The book does not go into tactical project selection, but a robust strategy goes a long way to helping make these tactical decisions).

Wrap-Up

Doing business without a strategy is like engaging in battle without a plan. Our major benchmarking study's results strongly support this adage. So do other investigations. Clearly, those businesses that lack goals for their total new product effort, where arenas of strategic focus have not been defined, and where the strategy is little more than a short term list of projects (no strategic product roadmap), are at a decided disadvantage.

Do what the top performers do. Set goals and objectives for your business's product innovation effort (e.g., the percentage of sales from new products). Tie your goals for product innovation firmly to your business's goals. And make these goals clear to everyone involved in your organization.

You can emulate the best performers by specifying strategic arenas. These are areas of strategic focus defined in terms of markets, technologies and product-types or categories. And map out your attack strategies: how you plan to enter and win in each arena.

Then consider going several steps further. Move toward strategic buckets and decide priorities and spending splits across these arenas, and spending splits across other strategic dimensions. These will be your deployment decisions. Lastly, develop strategic product roadmaps that lay out the direction of your major development initiatives over the next few years.

In the next chapters, we begin the journey of how to develop some of these strategic elements and how to craft them into a winning product innovation strategy for your business . . . so read on!

CHAPTER 2

Goals and Objectives

A goal properly set is halfway reached.

Abraham Lincoln

Setting Your Goals and Objectives

You may have seen the cartoon of a group of inebriated fellows in a rowboat at night in the fog. The cartoon shows one fellow shining a flashlight ahead without any clue as to where they're headed, but urging his mates to "row harder". The caption reads: "Having lost sight of our goals, we re-doubled our efforts", which is exactly what we see too many firms and executive teams doing. Their goals are unclear, so they make up the deficiency by working harder or running faster – heroic efforts that may yield results in the short term, but usually don't get you to where you want to be in the long-run. Product innovation goals provide direction for your business's total new product development effort. Clear goals give everyone in your organization a sense of purpose – where you are headed.

In setting goals for your business's product innovation effort, note that goals can be broad or general in nature; they do not have to be specific enough to act on, but should give one a future target or direction. And they must flow from, or be closely linked to, your overall business strategy, and thus are decided by the leadership team of the business. Examples of goals for product innovation:

- To leverage our innovation capabilities to yield a steady stream of breakthrough new products that will make us the industry leader in product development.
- To be recognized as the industry innovator – delivering new superior products of uncompromised quality that delight our customers.

Goals and Objectives for Product Innovation

Many people use the terms "goals" and "objectives" interchangeably. But there are important differences between the two. Generally speaking…

- Goals are broad whereas objectives are narrow
- Goals give general intentions; objectives are more precise
- Goals tend to be intangible; objectives are tangible
- Goals are abstract; objectives are concrete
- Goals cannot be validated easily; objectives can be validated.

Thus, in contrast to goals, the *objectives* for product innovation should be clear and concise: they must be SMART objectives to accomplish the

- **Objectives for your business's Product Innovation…**
  - Are the ultimate criteria for making decisions
  - Are the basis for your planning and strategy development
  - Provide consistency to your strategy's many elements
  - Yield a sense of purpose for those that must implement the strategy (e.g. the project teams, middle management, gatekeepers)
  - Provide benchmarks against which to measure performance

- **Innovation Objectives must be SMART:**
  - Specific
  - Measurable (hence be quantifiable)
  - Action-oriented
  - Realistic (achievable, but still a bit of a stretch)
  - Time-frame

- **Most importantly, your business's product innovation objectives…**
  - Must be understood by all (simply stated and communicated)

EXHIBIT 2.1: Defining objectives is the starting point in the development of your business's Product Innovation Strategy.

goals you set for your business's total product innovation effort (Exhibit 2.1).

What does SMART mean? Objectives should be *Specific;* that is, sufficiently detailed so as to be operational. In order for the objectives to be *Measurable,* they should be quantifiable (objectives provide clear targets against which you can measure your business's performance). *Action-oriented* objectives point to the tasks that need to be done. Objectives should be *Realistic* but challenging – a bit of a stretch to achieve. And objectives should have a *Time-frame* attached in order to be timely. Examples of objectives for product innovation:

- To increase revenue from new products from the current 14 percent to 30 percent by the end of year three.
- To increase the number of major new product launches from one annually to three per year (a major new product being one that creates a minimum of $2 million in sales after year three).

Example: The quest for measurability is not as straightforward as one might imagine. In one consumer products firm, the business unit leader declared that, "We want new products to increase our market share in this market by 1.5 times over the next five years." But what was the current market share, he was asked. There was an uncomfortable pause. "We're not really sure – that category is ill-defined, and we don't have good numbers on the current market size." So how can you set objectives in terms of market share when you cannot even measure the size of the market? The message is: Make sure when you set objectives that you really can measure the results. A more useful objective here might have been, "To increase sales by 1.5 times through new products" – an internal number that can be easily measured.

Why Have Objectives At All?

Defining objectives for product innovation is hard work. Yet every strategic plan always has a section entitled "Objectives". Why bother? Simple:

- Objectives are the ultimate criteria for making decisions. Many decisions will be made in the design and implementation of your innovation strategy; and clear objectives are the foundation of that decision making. For example, the simple question in a strategy meeting: "Does focusing on this market help us achieve our objective?" cannot be answered without having clear objectives and an understanding of it.

- Objectives are the basis for planning and strategy development. The whole point of crafting a plan or strategy is to achieve an objective. Recall from Chapter 1, the first principle in the US Army Field Manual: "Objective: direct every military operation toward a clearly defined, decisive, and attainable objective". This rings true for product innovation too.

- Objectives provide for consistency among the elements of your innovation strategy. There are many components of an innovation strategy (as well as the dozens of tactics needed to implement the strategy), and clear objectives are the glue that hold these potentially disparate pieces together.

- Objectives provide a sense of purpose for the people who have to implement the strategy and plans; for example the project teams, middle managers and gatekeeper groups.

- Finally, objectives provide benchmarks against which to measure the new product performance of the business. This is important, because benchmarking – measuring where you are versus where you should be – tells you whether or not you are off course, and when serious corrective action is needed.

Most Businesses Lack Clearly Defined Objectives

Defining objectives for your product innovation strategy is essential. Most business leaders accept that premise. But our major benchmarking investigation revealed that almost two-thirds of companies lack written and measurable objectives for their innovation effort (Exhibit 1.3 in

Chapter 1). In our work with clients, we see this played out over and over. Consider the two examples that follow.

Example 1: A senior executive was about to kickoff a strategy-crafting session for his organization, hoping that this would be a good way to get the involvement and engagement of all his senior people. As host and lead-off speaker, he embarked on a discussion of objectives, and then paused, asking each senior person to write down the business's objective for product innovation. These submissions were then collected and read aloud. The trouble was no two were the same! By the time the senior executive read the fourth submission, folks were snickering and laughing out loud. The executive team was quick to acknowledge that each senior person had a different view of the business's objectives for product development. Not a good beginning point. Objectives had not been clearly delineated nor communicated.

Example 2: At a product innovation strategy meeting in a large business unit within a major conglomerate, the question was asked, "What are your objectives for product innovation?" and the answer came back in unison: "15 in 5". Somewhat taken aback by the loud and uniform response, we asked what this meant. One executive explained, "The objective is clear – Within the next five years, we will launch 15 major new products. A major product is defined as one that will put $1 million dollars on the bottom line in year three".

You may disagree with the objective in Example 2, or criticize it for being too simple, but the point is that the objective was loud and clear, easy to understand, and communicated to all who needed to know. It was also specific, measurable, action-oriented and realistic with a specified time-frame. In the days that followed, in meetings with lower level people, we asked the same question, "What are your objectives?" and the answer was always the same: "15 in 5". It was as though every new product employee – technical, marketing and operations – had stamped "15 in 5" on their forehead and looked at it in the mirror every morning. Everyone was marching to the same drummer.

Incidentally, the business unit achieved the objective handily.

Measurement and Metrics

Objectives are benchmarks against which to measure performance. For this to occur a close-looped feedback system must exist to provide for real-time course corrections and, over time, generates *continuous improvement*. The model, illustrated in Exhibit 2.2, illustrates that you must set objectives, formulate strategy and action plans, execute these plans, then measure performance against the original objectives. If the objectives are not met, then corrective action needs to occur; perhaps the objectives were unrealistic in the first place, which calls for setting new and more realistic objectives; or, perhaps the actions were wrong. Maybe the strategy

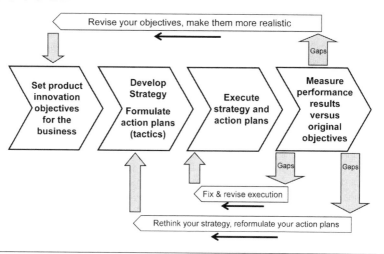

EXHIBIT 2.2: Setting objectives for innovation, and then measuring performance against them, creates a continuous improvement, closed loop feedback model.

or the tactical plans were inappropriate, or they were poorly executed. Any of these negative results would call for a revise-and-rethink.

Objectives are closely linked to *performance metrics*. Indeed, consistent with the principle that "what gets measured gets done", the popular metrics that companies use to measure new product performance provide a useful guide to selecting appropriate objectives – see Exhibit 2.3. (Note that the numbers in Exhibit 2.3 add to more than 100 percent because most businesses use more than one performance metric.)

Here note that more than two-thirds of businesses (68.6 percent) rely on "percent of sales from new products" as a performance metric. Within a company, this might be stated as, "Thirty percent of our current annual sales came from new products we launched within the last three years." Another popular metric is the percentage of growth in sales from new products. Half of all companies use this measure – for example, "new products launched in the previous three years accounted for 72 percent of our sales growth this past year." About one third of companies use "percentage of business's profits from new products" as an important

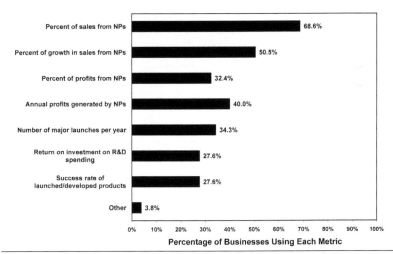

EXHIBIT 2.3: A number of metrics are used to gauge the overall performance of total product innovation efforts, with "percentage of sales from new products" (NPs) the most popular by far.

performance measure. For example, "new products generated $12.5 million in profits for our business for the last fiscal year."

Typical Performance Metrics Results

Benchmarking other firms and their innovation performance can help set product development objectives for your own company. Exhibit 2.4 shows typical performance results, broken down by the best, average and worst performing firms. Some relevant benchmarking results to consider in setting your own objectives:

- Percentage of revenue coming from new products: The most popular metric; on average, 27.5 percent of sales come from new products launched in the previous three years. But this percentage varies considerably: from a high of 38 percent for the best one-fifth of firms to a low of nine percent for the bottom one-fifth. This number also varies greatly by industry.
- Percentage of projects meeting profit objectives: A second metric, and one that is a good objective, is the recovered profit – that is, how profitable your new products actually are versus the projections made in the business cases when they were approved for development. Here, just over half of development projects meet their profit objectives. In the case of best performers, the proportion rises to almost four out of five projects on target.

Example: Procter & Gamble tracks the profits achieved by its new products (measured by NPV) versus the forecast profits as shown in the business case. In the mid-to-late 1990s, this performance ratio (actual profits to forecast profits, or "success rate" as they call it) was less than 50 percent; that is, less than half the forecasted profits from new products were actually realized.

As might be expected, driving the success rate up – from less than 50 percent to 75 percent – became one vital objective.[1] One reason for poor performance had been overzealous forecasts by project leaders

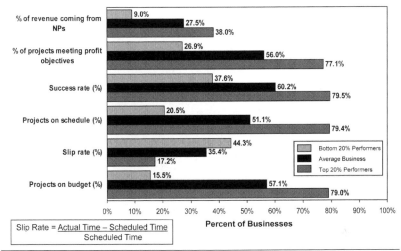

EXHIBIT 2.4: Bar charts show how businesses typically perform in product innovation on popular metrics, with the best, average and worst performers noted.

desirous of promoting their own projects. Other issues were poor execution and weak follow-through after launch. Today, with the right actions taken (for example, holding project teams accountable for results in the marketplace and solidifying the use of P&G's robust SIMPL stage-and-gate process), the success rate, or recovered profits, now approach 80 percent – well above the 75 percent objective.[2]

Other popular metrics in Exhibit 2.4 that might translate into useful product innovation objectives deal with time-to-market, on budget performance and the "slip rate". The slip rate is a very useful relative time metric that captures actual cycle time (time from project approval to launch date) measured against the promised or scheduled cycle time. Note that the average business achieves a slip rate of 35 percent; that is, the product is promised in 12 months from approval date, but the actual development and launch take 16 months. Best performers achieve a remarkable 17 percent slip rate – 12 months is promised, and they get there in 13 months. What's your slip rate? And should an improvement here be an objective for new products in your business?

Percentage of sales is the most popular performance metric, but is it the best? Although percentage of sales is the most popular metric in Exhibits 2.3 and 2.4, be aware that it is not necessarily the best metric to gauge performance. This metric was popularized by 3M and other firms who held general managers and other senior executives in their business units accountable for achieving a certain percentage of sales annually from new products. But here are words of warning from an astute and experienced CTO in our benchmarking study:[3]

"Percentage of sales is a 'good news, bad news' metric. One of our business units has a very high percentage of sales from new products. But this is due to a *combination of negative factors*: high and costly product obsolesce in their market; new products that did not perform – either technically or financially – and needed to be fixed and replaced (and hence were double-counted); and over-reaction to every single customer request. The result is a lot of unnecessary 'churn' in the product line, which is very costly to the business. So a high percentage of sales is not always a good thing."

Thus, percentage of sales may not be the best performance metric. Indeed achieving a high percentage of sales may be the result of poor and costly new product practices, as in the example above! This metric may also motivate the wrong kind of behavior; for example, in one business we were working with, the general manager simply changed the definition of a "new product" so that anything requiring an engineering drawing – even the smallest changes – was counted as a new product. In yet another firm, senior people went through the list of "old products" in their catalogue (existing products that had not been sold for more than three years) to see which ones could be easily replaced, so that their business could "make the numbers" and hit the new product percentage of sales target. This practice lead to unnecessary cannibalization (or premature obsolesce) of existing and very profitable products.

Defining a New Product

One of the challenges with setting objectives for product innovation and measuring performance is defining what is meant by a new product. Most of the metrics and objectives above rely on a tight definition of new products in order to be effective. Many instances exist where weak or vague definitions have allowed management to "play with the numbers"; for example, count initiatives as new products that are probably not. So, before you establish objectives for product innovation and formulate metrics to gauge performance, it is important to agree on a robust definition of what is a "new product".

What is a product: First, let's be clear about what we mean by "product". For you, a product is anything that your firm offers to the external marketplace for sale or consumption in return for compensation. Products include physical products as well as service offerings and combinations of these. But freebies – for example, providing free servicing or free training programs – do not count as products. That is simply customer service or marketing and is a cost of doing business. But if you charged money for that training program, then it's a product. Nor do internal developments count; such as an internal IT group developing a new sales reporting system for internal use. If it does not directly generate external revenue, it is not a product. Similarly, an R&D lab develops an improved production process that increases yield in the plant – it's a valuable project, but is not a new product! (Note that many of the principles of effective new product management can be applied to these internal projects, but for purposes of setting and measuring objectives for product innovation, they are not new products per se.)

What is New: Now for the definition of the "new" part of "new product". This is a little more difficult, but nonetheless important if you are to set objectives and measure results. There are many different types of "new" products; indeed "newness" can be defined in terms of two dimensions:

- *New to the company*, in the sense that your business has never made or sold this type of product before, but other companies might have. Nonetheless you must still incur the costs of development and launch, and face the risks associated with a new initiative.
- *New to the market* or, in the extreme, "a true innovation": Here the product is the first of its kind on the market. This is the traditional definition of "new product"; but if you adhered to this definition alone, you would exclude much of the product development effort that takes place within your business.

Categories of New Products

On the two-dimensional map shown in Exhibit 2.5, six different types or classes of new products are illustrated:

1. *New-to-the-world products:* These new products are the first of their kind and create an entirely new market (upper right corner of Exhibit 2.5). This category represents only 10 percent of all new products.[4] Well known examples include the Sony Walkman, Pfizer's Viagra, and 3M's Post-It Notes.

2. *New product lines:* These products, although not new to the marketplace, are nonetheless totally new to your business (upper left corner of Exhibit 2.5). About 20 percent of all new products fit into this category. They allow a company to enter an established market for the first time. For example, Apple was not the first to market a portable MP3 player (although one might argue, they were the first to launch a totally integrated MP3 system that was easy to use); the Korean firm, Saehan Information Systems, was the first with their MPMan in 1993, eight years earlier than Apple. When Apple did introduce its version, it was clearly not an innovation, but it did represent a significantly better product and certainly a new product line for Apple, with all the investment requirements that entailed.

3. *Additions to existing product lines:* These are new items to your business, but fit within an existing product line that you already make

or sell. They may also represent a fairly new product to the market-place. An example is Hewlett-Packard's next model in its *LaserJet* line, a more up-to-date and more powerful version of its laser printers. The printer is a new item within the *LaserJet* line, and its added features make it somewhat novel or "new to the market." Such new items are one of the largest categories of new products – about 26 percent of all new product launches.

4. *Improvements and revisions to existing products:* These "not-so-new" products are essentially replacements of existing products in your business's existing product line. They offer improved performance or greater perceived value over the "old" product. These "new and improved" products also make up 26 percent of all new product launches. For example, when P&G launches a "new and improved" detergent or a fabric softener with a new fragrance, these are essentially improvements, revisions and extensions of existing product lines. In business-to-business (B2B) marketing for example, ExxonMobil Chemicals produces modified polyolefin plastics. A significant

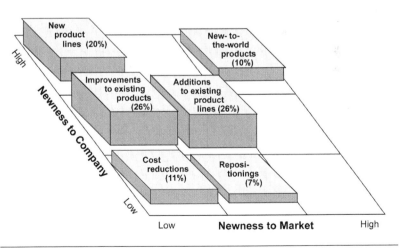

EXHIBIT 2.5: Define what is a "new product". There are two dimensions of newness; new to the company (vertical) and new to the market (horizontal).

percentage of its R&D effort goes into product "tweaks"; that is, modifying existing polymers in order to respond to a changing customer requirement or a competitive threat.

5. *Repositionings:* These are essentially new applications for your existing products, and often involve retargeting an old product at a new market segment or for a different application. For years, Bayer's Aspirin (or ASA, as it is known in some countries) was the standard headache, pain and fever reliever. Superseded by newer, safer classes of drugs such as non-steroidal anti-inflammatory drugs (NSAID); Aspirin was in trouble. But new medical evidence suggested that Aspirin had other benefits. Now Aspirin is positioned, not just as a headache pill, but as a blood thinner – a blood clot, stroke, and heart attack preventer. Repositionings account for about 7 percent of all new products.

6. *Cost reductions:* These are the least "new" of all new product categories. They are new products designed to replace existing ones in your product line, but yield similar benefits and performance at lower cost. For example, the product may have been redesigned to make it simpler, or to use lower cost components, thus rendering it cheaper to produce. From a marketing and customer standpoint, this is not a new product (indeed the marketing people hope the changes are almost invisible to the consumer); but from a design and production viewpoint, they could represent a significant technical undertaking. These cost reduction new products make up 11 percent of all new product launches. (Note that these should not be confused with internal "process developments" which are improvements to the operations process, but do not result in a new product).

The two most popular categories – additions to existing product lines and product improvements or revisions – are common to almost all firms. By contrast, the "step-out" products – new-to-the-world and new-to-the-company product lines – constitute only 30 percent of all new product launches, but represent 60 percent of the products viewed as "most successful".[5] Best performing businesses appear to undertake a much higher proportion of these innovative projects: They represent over 40 percent of the development portfolios in best performing firms.[6] In Chapter 5, where the topic is portfolio management and strategic buckets, we gain more insight into the right balance and mix of projects.

Most companies use the top four categories in Exhibit 2.5 – the upper two-thirds of the matrix – when they define "new products" in their product development objectives and metrics. These include "new to the world", "new to the company", "additions to existing product lines", and "significant product improvements". But "cost reductions" and "repositions" are usually not counted as new products.

Beyond Traditional Definitions of New Products

Most of the metrics above (hence the objectives connected to them) require a definition of "new product", which can be problematic. For example, defining what is a "significant improvement" can lead to shades of gray. Here are some ways to deal with the problems in defining "what counts as a new product?" when using the popular metrics "percentage of sales by new products", and similar metrics such as "percentage of growth by new products", or "profits generated from new products" – indeed any of the metrics that require a solid definition of "new product" in order to be useful.

A few companies now adopt a *much tighter and more narrow definition* of new products. Parker Hannifin, for example, defines "new products" to include only "new-to-the-world" and "new-to-the-market" products. Significant improvements, new items in an existing product line, cost reductions, modifications and tweaks shown in Exhibit 2.5 are simply not counted in their performance metrics or objectives.[7] This certainly makes the definition of "new product" a lot easier to operationalize. The argument here is that truly innovative products – new-to-the-world and new-to-the-market – are the ones that Parker Hannifin is seeking in order to drive the growth of their businesses. By contrast, the other development efforts – modifications, improvements and new items – are simply sustaining innovation and are thus the cost of doing business, but not really new products in this company's eyes.

Similarly, ITT Industries had to deal with the issue of which projects to count as new. It has tightened the definition to include only products "with new features, functionality and benefits, that are clearly visible to the customer or user, and involving an engineering spend of at least $50,000". The notion here is that the "new" product must be new in the eyes of the customer and, at the same time, entail some risk to ITT itself.

Another way to tighten the definition of "new products" is to count only incremental sales. Thus, replacement products, or improvements that generate no additional revenue, or new products that cannibalize the sales of an existing product would not count – unless the sales are incremental or in addition to existing sales. For example, MARS Petfoods uses net incremental sales value (NSV) as the key metric. This "incremental sales" definition certainly fosters the right behavior (no more unnecessary and expensive churn in the product portfolio); unless the product generates new business, it doesn't count. And this metric encourages the quest for new products that are more innovative and offense-oriented, designed to gain new business and sales. One added bonus is that measuring incremental sales is more quantifiable and exact than attempting to decide whether or not "new functionality is visible to the customer". Hence, the metric is more operational and reliable than most.

Setting Your Product Innovation Objectives

Types of High-Level Objectives to Consider

What types of objectives should be included in an innovation strategy? Many firms enunciate one or two high level objectives for their business overall, and then a few lower level or sub-objectives that flow from these. Higher level objectives that are typically seen as part of an innovation strategy have already been mentioned above. Here are some recommendations regarding their use (see Exhibit 2.6 for a summary):

1. *The percentage of sales* that will be derived from new products introduced in the previous three year period. For example: "By the year 2012, the target is for 32 percent of annual sales to come from new products launched in the previous three years."

Three years is a generally accepted time span in which to define a product as "new," although given today's pace of business, two years may be more appropriate for many businesses such as electronics and high-tech. In contrast, five years is often used in industries where the market adoption rate is very slow, and it may take many years for new products' sales to ramp up. In addition, the year of introduction is often not counted, as the product does not benefit from a full year of sales the first year.

Alternatively, one can speak of absolute sales; that is, the sales dollars coming from new products, rather than the percentages. For example: "This 32 percent translates into $50 million in sales in 2012 from new products launched in the previous three years."

Also recommended is the use of *absolute dollar sales* from new products in conjunction with percentage of sales. Both come from the same calculation, but are different ways of saying the same thing. Percentage of sales is particularly useful for comparison – to your industry, to other business units, and to previous years; while dollar sales is a little more concrete for your own people.

The recommendation is that you utilize *percentage of sales by new products* when defining your business's product innovation objectives. It's popular: it has stood the test of time; for the most part, it encourages the right behavior; it is fairly measurable and operational; and, there are data to benchmark your business against. But recognize its weaknesses too. Be sure to consider a tighter definition of "what constitutes a new product" so that this objective encourages and rewards the right behavior. And do consider other metrics as objectives as well. The percentage of sales statistic, as a metric and as an objective, is far from perfect and cannot do the job alone.

2. *The percentage of profits* that will be derived from new products introduced during a given time span also works as an objective. For example: "By the year 2012, the target is that 30 percent of our businesses EBIT will come from new products launched in the previous three years." Again, absolute dollar profits can be used as well as a percentage.

Note that while new product profits (not sales) is usually the ultimate objective, profits from new products may be more difficult to measure. For example, do you subtract a portion of R&D costs from your new product profits, or are these R&D costs simply treated as overhead? And how do you handle the cost of shared production equipment between old products and new products? Additionally, your business's annual profits (the denominator in the percentage of profits calculation) are less stable year-to-year than are sales, so the percentage of profits is likely to bounce around a lot. For these reasons, we caution you about using this profit metric as an objective.

Recommended types of high level product innovation objectives:
1. Percentage of sales by new products (launched in last 3 years) in Year X
2. Dollar sales from new products in Year X
3. Net or incremental sales from new products – for objectives 1 and 2
4. Sales objectives from NPs as a percentage of sales growth
5. The strategic role of new products:
    - Defending your market share
    - Exploiting a new technology
    - Establishing a foothold in a new market
    - Opening up a new technological or market window of opportunity
    - Capitalizing on a strength or resource
    - Diversifying into higher-growth areas

Lower level objectives:
1. Success, failure and kill rates of development projects (e.g. recovered profit)
2. Minimum acceptable financial returns for projects
3. Number of new product ideas per year
4. Number of (major) launches per year
5. Number of projects entering development per year

EXHIBIT 2.6: Use these different types of innovation objectives as a guide. Be sure to have a very robust definition of what constitutes a "new product".

3. Sales and profits from new products expressed as a percentage of business growth. For example: "70 percent of our growth in sales over the next three years will come from new products introduced in this period." These are similar metrics to items 1 and 2 above, but expressed in a different and, perhaps, more meaningful way. For example, this measure firmly ties your business objective (business growth) to your new product objectives. Again, the use of sales rather than profits may be more practical. Thus, the recommendation is the use of new product sales as a percentage of growth in sales objective and metric in conjunction with the more popular percentage of sales.

Example: A major manufacturer of machine tool controls has sales of $70 million. Its business goal is to double sales over a five year period. The expectation is that three-quarters of this growth will come from new products (the other one-quarter will come from other sources such as new markets or market growth).

Now do the math – see Exhibit 2.7; doubling the $70M sales figure in five years is a compounded rate just under 15 percent annually (current or base year is 2009; target year is 2014).

Objectives for new products now become much more concrete:

- Three quarters of the business's sales growth is to come from new products – that is, new products play the dominant role in the growth plan.
- This means that the new product sales objective in 2012 (launched that year and in the previous two years) is $27.1 million.
- And in 2014 (the target year), the new product sales objective increases to $35.8 million.
- In percentages, this means that the objective for new product sales is 25.6 percent of the annual sales for each year, 2012 to 2014.

4. Return on investment of RD&E funds spent. This is a worthwhile objective, as it is a productivity metric or objective: output over input or "bang for buck". In short, this objective has the goal of maximizing (or

Year	Base Year 09	2010	2011	2012	2013	2014
Company Sales Goal ($M)	70.0%	80.4%	92.4%	106.2%	122.0%	140.0% (double)
Annual Sales Increase ($M)	-	10.4%	12.0%	13.8%	15.8%	18.2%
75% to come from NPs ($M)	-	7.8%	9.0%	10.3%	11.9%	13.6%
Sales from NP – last 3 years ($M)				27.1%	31.2%	35.8%
% Sales from NPs – last 3 years (%)				25.6%	25.6%	25.6%

EXHIBIT 2.7: Objectives for new products can be set by tying them to the company's overall growth goal. Here the growth goal is to double the business in five years, with 75% of this growth coming from new products.

hitting a certain target) in terms of what profit is achieved for the funds spent. Operationally, the objective and metric are calculated as follows:

$$ROI = \frac{\text{Profits from new products (launched last X years)}}{\text{RD\&E funds spent on new products}}$$

While admirable conceptually, the objective is fraught with operational problems. As noted above, measuring profits from new products has many difficulties: which initiatives do you count; do you count incremental profits only; and how do you deal with the cost of shared resources, such as a production facility or a salesforce? The denominator in this equation is similarly plagued: Do you count all RD&E costs incurred by the business, or only that portion spent on new products (which may be hard to split off)? And what about other costs incurred by new products? It is estimated that RD&E may be less than half the total cost of product development; there are also marketing, sales, operations and senior management time and costs to be considered. All of these are more difficult to determine. For these reasons, we cannot recommend

ROI on RD&E spending as an objective or meaningful metric. There are just too many problems in its measurement.

5. *The strategic role of product innovation* is very often a more difficult goal to quantify, but can be useful as a goal for product innovation. These types of objectives include: Defending market share; exploiting a new technology; establishing a foothold in a new market; opening up a new technological or market window of opportunity; capitalizing on a strength or resource; or diversifying into higher-growth areas. These types of qualitative goals, when used in conjunction with more quantifiable objectives cited above, provide a useful addition to the possible quantifiable objectives you should consider.

Types of Lower-Level Objectives to Consider

Certain lower-level objectives flow logically from the product innovation objectives outlined and recommended above. For example, if the business wants 70 percent of sales growth to come from new products, how does that figure translate into the number of successful products; number of development projects; success, failure, and kill rates; and number of ideas to be considered annually? Thus, a number of possible lower-level objectives should be considered, such as:

- *Success, failure, and kill rates of new products developed.* Recall the earlier P&G example in Chapter 1 where management set a target to increase the success rate (recovered profit) from less than 50 percent to 75 percent. This was a lower-level thought process that was necessary to achieve their desired percentage-of-sales objective.
- *Increasing the financial returns for new product projects* (or hitting some minimal target). The goal is similar to the success rate cited just above, and involves tracking the ROI or IRR of new products launched each year.
- *The number of new product ideas to be generated or considered annually.* For example, Swarovski, a maker and retailer of high-end

crystal and jewelry, set 66 percent of sales from new products as the objective for new products in their global consumer business.[8] This translates into hundreds of new consumer jewelry and crystal items annually. To achieve this, Swarovski's Vice President of Innovation set a target of 500 new ideas to be generated annually from a new internal ideation capture and handling system called I-Flash. After less than three years in operation, over 1,300 ideas have been collected, and 650 employees have participated; further, while some ideas did not progress, a total of 3,000 evaluations have been undertaken by expert evaluators within the company.

- *The number of new products to be introduced annually.* An example of this was shown earlier in the chapter, the goal of "15 in 5" or "fifteen major new products to be launched in the next five years". There are problems with this type of objective, however. Products could be large-volume or small-volume ones (in this example, the general manager had specified the minimum acceptable size of product), and the number of products does not directly translate into sales and profits. Nonetheless, when used in conjunction with one of the higher level objectives – such as percentage of sales or growth to be achieved from new products – this objective and metric works. For one thing, it is clear and can be communicated and easily understood.

- *The number of projects entering development (or in development) annually.* Like the number of products to be launched or number of ideas to be considered annually, this objective is often an outgrowth of a pipeline analysis: "If your objective is $10 million dollars in sales from new products annually, how many launches, how many development projects, and how many ideas does that translate into annually?" Recognize that there is an attrition curve – that many ideas are needed to spawn a single development project, and a number of development projects may be needed to yield a successful launch. Exhibit 2.8 shows an average attrition curve, based on Product Development Management Association (PDMA) data.[9]

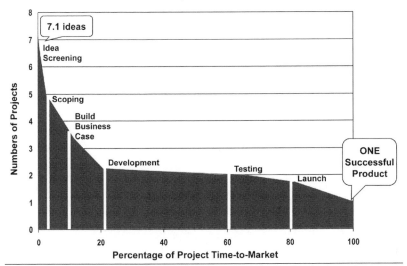

EXHIBIT 2.8: When setting objectives in terms of numbers of major launches annually, do not forget the attrition curve – you will need more development projects to get that one winner, and lots of ideas.

Some Guidance – Types of Objectives by Business Strategy

When thinking about what types of objectives might serve your own business best, sometimes looking at the different objectives found in similar companies provides some guidance. A study of many businesses employing different innovation strategies reveals that the types of objectives employed vary considerably, and depend to some extent on what strategy each company employs (Exhibit 2.9).[10]

The Innovators: The industry innovators are often called the "prospectors" or "pioneers." They value being first-in to the market with new products and technologies, and they respond rapidly to early signals pointing to new opportunities. The following types of objectives are common to these businesses:

- Percentage of profits from new products
- Percentage of sales from new products
- The ability to open up new windows of opportunity.

Fast Followers: These enterprises, sometimes called "analyzers", carefully monitor the actions of innovative competitors. When they spot competitive activity, such as a successful new product launch, they move quickly to copy and enhance upon the pioneer's product, often launching a better product than the pioneer. In terms of product innovation objectives, these fast follower firms tend to look for:

- ROI (return-on-investment) from development efforts
- Whether the innovation effort fits or supports the business's overall strategy
- Percentage of profits from new products
- Success/failure rates.

The Defenders: Defender organizations attempt to maintain secure positions or niches in stable areas. They protect their domain by offering higher quality or lower prices, or they rely on some other element of the marketing mix, such as broad distribution or superb

1. **Innovators – prospector businesses – use:**
   - Percentage of profits from new products
   - Percentage of sales from new products
   - Ability to open up new windows of opportunity
2. **Fast followers – analyzer enterprises looking for competitive advantage – use:**
   - ROI (return-on-investment) from development efforts
   - Whether the innovation effort fits or supports the business's overall strategy
   - Percentage of profits from new products
   - Success/failure rates
3. **Defender organizations use:**
   - ROI from development efforts
   - Fit with, or support of, the business's strategy
   - Market share protection
   - Gross margin improvements
4. **Reactor businesses use:**
   - ROI from development efforts
   - Success/failure rates
   - Fits with, or support of, the business's strategy
   - Market share maintenance

EXHIBIT 2.9: Firms with different strategies tend of have different types of innovation goals. Which strategy type are you?

customer relationships. Product innovation is not front-and-center in their business strategy. Their product innovation objectives tend to be:

- ROI from development efforts
- Fit with or support of the business's strategy
- Market share protection
- Gross margin improvements.

Reactors: Reactor businesses are characterized by a "non strategy" when it comes to product innovation. They are not as aggressive in maintaining established products and markets, and respond only when forced to. They are slow to develop new products, and tend to be very reactive to competitors and to external forces. Their implicit objectives for product innovation are:

- ROI from development efforts
- Success/failure rates
- Fit with or support of the business's strategy
- Market share maintenance.

How to Set Your Business's Product Innovation Objectives

Setting your objectives is no easy task. The first time through, the exercise is often a frustrating experience. Yet these objectives are fundamental to developing an innovation strategy, not to mention a logically determined R&D spending figure. Some recommended approaches are described below:

Competitive Parity or Competitive Leadership

Benchmark yourself against the average and the best in your industry. Looking at industry averages and at leading firms in your industry provides a guide to setting your own objectives. Since percentage of sales is by far the most popular metric, logically this becomes the measure to use when setting objectives by benchmarking other firms.

The concept here is that the average firm provides a reasonable and attainable standard against which to perform (and hence to set objectives), especially if your business is below that average. But the top performers' metrics are the ones to aspire to for the longer term.

Example: In 2002, ITT Industries achieved only 15 percent of sales from new products launched in the previous three years (Exhibit 2.10).[11] Desirous of improving their innovation efforts, and to respond to calls for improved Price/Earnings ratio by shareholders, a "Value Based Product Development" task force was set up. The initial objective was to match their industry average, namely 28 percent of sales from new products. This meant almost doubling the innovation

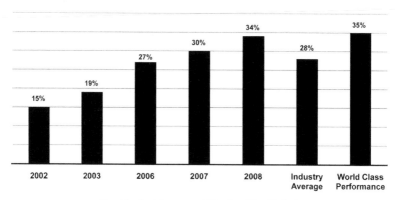

New Product Revenue Objective (% of Sales)

EXHIBIT 2.10: The competitive parity approach requires that you benchmark your results against those of the average firm in your industry and against the best performers. This company began at 15% in 2002 and set an immediate objective to double their performance to match the industry average in five years (which they did). The next goal was to climb to the best performers within seven years.

rate within five years. The longer term objective was to match the industry's best performers within seven years (35 percent sales by new products), which they are very close to achieving now.

One of the problems with this approach is that it is difficult to find reliable data against which to benchmark yourself. Exhibit 2.11 does provide some guidance here, showing percentage of sales from new products launched within the last three years for a wide variety of industries. Note that this metric is very industry dependent, so be sure to select the industry that comes closest to yours when using data in this table. The term "new products" used here includes all types of new products from significant changes and modifications through to true innovations.

Gap Analysis

Here, new product objective setting usually begins with a strategic planning exercise for the entire business. Growth and profit goals are decided, along

Industry	New Product Sales as % of Total Revenue
FMCG	24%
Capital	26%
Consumer Services	25%
Industrial Services	21%
Chemicals	18%
Other Materials	20%
Healthcare	31%
Technology	47%
Software and Services	45%

Source: PDMA Foundation & Marjorie Adams, 2004

EXHIBIT 2.11: Industry differences – new product sales as a percentage of total revenue. How does your company compare to the industry average?

with the business's overall strategy. These goals and thrusts are then translated into new product objectives via gap analysis. The method is outlined in Exhibit 2.12.

In gap analysis, one creates two plots:

- *Desired state:* What you desire your business's sales (or profits) to be over the next 3-5 years, based on your overall business goals. Often this is set by the corporate head office or the shareholders and owners.
- *Expected state:* What the expected sales (or profits) will likely be, assuming the current product lines and their status quo strategy. This means making forecasts of current products and lines and their life cycle curves, without strategic changes envisioned. Thus, the forecast is what probably will occur – the "expected state" – unless you alter your strategy.

Steps in Gap Analysis
- **Plot expected revenues and profits over time with current strategy: the expected (or probable) state**
- **Plot what sales and profits should be, according to business goals (e.g. growth): the desired state**
- **Look at the gap. What will fill it?**
  - Increased market share with existing products?
  - Market growth?
  - New markets?
  - New products?
  - Acquisitions?

> There is only a limited number of ways to fill the gap.
> Define the role that NPD will play – in $000 or %.

EXHIBIT 2.12: In setting product innovation objectives for your business, use Gap Analysis – the difference being the desired state and expected state. Then determine what will fill the gap.

Usually there is a gap between the two projections – between the desired state and the expected state. And the gap gets larger the further one looks into the future. This gap must be filled, and there are only so many ways to do that: by new products, new markets, new businesses, market development, or market share increases (or acquisitions if that's within your strategic mandate). In this way, the objectives are decided for each of these efforts, including product development.

Example: Senior management at Guinness (Ireland) developed a strategic plan for their brewing business. Ambitious sales growth and profit objectives were decided and were driven by their parent company, Diageo in London. A review of current products and markets, however, revealed that a gap would exist between projected sales and the objectives (Exhibit 2.13). That is, current products and markets were projected into the future, and expected revenues and profits were compared to the desired level of sales and profits (the business objectives). This revealed a gap in expectations.

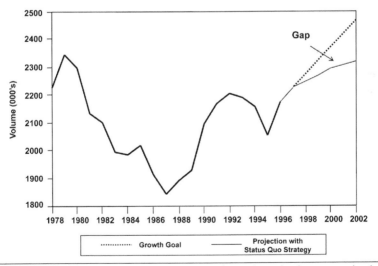

EXHIBIT 2.13: An example of Gap Analysis. Here the projected volumes starting in 1995 are shown with the current or "status quo" strategy and also the growth objective dictated by headquarters.

The gap needed to be filled by new markets, new products or new businesses. Since there was limited or no growth in the beer market; since Guinness's market shares were already high in their main markets; and, since there were limits on market expansion, new products came front-and-center as the major source by which Guinness management would fill the gap. It was a simple process of elimination. From this mental exercise by the executive team, a set of new product objectives were determined.

Example: Alcatel-Lucent Technologies in the US went through a process similar to Guinness. They mapped out sales projections for current products and product categories (Exhibit 2.14). Note how projections for their four major markets are made (left, Exhibit 2.14); and then expected market shares of each of these four markets are forecast (middle, Exhibit 2.14). Multiplying data from the two sets of curves yields expected sales (far right), which can then be compared to business's growth and sales objectives. From this exercise, Lucent's

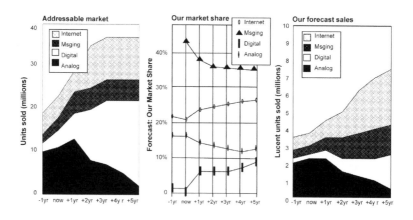

EXHIBIT 2.14: To determine the gap, look at your market size projections and then your market share projections (left, center). These yield the sales projections (right) for the four segments. Next, compare these to business objectives for total sales growth. The gap is easily identified.

management is able to spot shortfalls, which leads to the need for new products to fill the gaps, and hence their objectives for new products for the business.[12]

Once the gap between the expected sales and the desired sales is identified, then management must think strategically about ways to fill that gap. The trickle down model shown in Exhibit 2.15 provides a guide. Here management starts with the growth objective (a percent and a dollar figure), and makes estimates of how that growth objective will be achieved – what will fill the gap. There are only so many sources of growth (top left, Exhibit 2.15):

- Increased market size
- Increased share in existing markets
- Geographic expansion

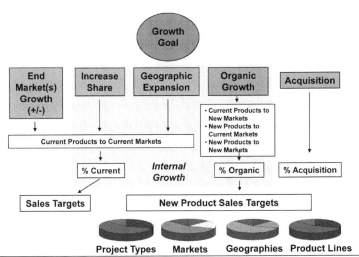

EXHIBIT 2.15: Use the trickle down model to define your innovation objectives. Start with growth goals and determine where this increase will come from. Insert dollars and percentages in the boxes. The objective for "Organic Growth" and ultimately "new products" falls out of this analysis.

- Organic growth: new market, new products
- Acquisitions.

Again, numbers are placed in the boxes as sources of growth – both percentages and dollar figures. And from this thought process, the dollar sales from new products (and new markets) over the foreseeable future are determined. The new product objectives are set!

Define Your Innovation Goals and Objectives: A Summary

Setting goals and objectives for your company's product innovation efforts is an important first step toward crafting your innovation strategy. But it is not as easy as it sounds. While goals can be broad and non-quantified, objectives must be SMART: specific, measurable, action-oriented, realistic and have a timeframe. Metrics that are typically used to gauge a business's new product performance are closely linked to objectives through a closed-loop feedback model. We recommend you take a look at popular metrics that are commonly used to measure product innovation performance. But note that even the popular metrics are problematic, suggesting that perhaps several different objectives should be used. And remember, before you define objectives, you must have a sharp and operational definition of what constitutes a "new product".

This chapter has outlined popular and sensible objectives to consider – both high-level as well as lower-level objectives that flow from the former. And different types of companies – innovators, fast followers, defenders and reactors – have been observed to use different types of objectives.

Finally, in setting objectives, competitive benchmarking provides a guide: How the average and top performing firms fare in your industry on key performance metrics, such as percentage of sales from new products. Finally, using a strategic approach – beginning with your business's goals and objectives and utilizing gap analysis and a trickle down model to define what role new products must play – is certainly recommended as a way to define your business's product innovation objectives.

CHAPTER 3

A Robust Strategic Analysis –
Key to Achieving the Right Focus

Tactics without strategy is the noise before defeat.

Sun Tzŭ c. 490 BC

Focus on the Right Strategic Arenas

The three most important things in developing an innovation strategy are focus, focus, and focus… but on the right Strategic Arenas! Too often, product development efforts resemble a scatter-gun approach: there is no focus; efforts are thinly spread across many fronts (different markets, technologies and product types); and there is little impact as a result. In military strategy, the principle of mass is vital; concentrate combat power at the decisive place and time. The same applies to innovation strategy.

Example: In one division of a major multinational conglomerate, the general manager was under pressure to produce new product results. His technical and marketing groups were very proficient, and typically executed new product projects effectively and on time. But something was missing. His boss, the president of the Division, made an insightful comment: "You guys are great at product development. The trouble is, you've never done anything twice... you're all over the place!" And he was right. A more careful analysis of past projects revealed that no two were similar or synergistic – different markets, different product types, and different applications. As the marketing executive declared: "We've never said no to an opportunity". This may be admirable entrepreneurial management – something this firm does not want to lose – but it certainly makes for an unfocused and low impact new product effort.

Recall from Chapter 1 that focus is one of the four most vital strategic themes leading to high performance in innovation.

In order to focus one's efforts, however, one must first answer the question: focus where? That means undertaking a careful strategic analysis of the options – the various strategic arenas and their relative attractiveness, coupled with the firm's capability to succeed in each arena. That's what this chapter is about. The military analogy also applies here: Picture a group of Generals in a war-room, trying to map out a strategy. They have limited resources in terms of troops and equipment and know that if they attack on too many fronts, they will dissipate their scarce resources and achieve minimal impact. One of the most important strategic decisions they face is where to attack – on which battlefields, fronts or Strategic Arenas to concentrate their effort. Many famous military battles have been lost because the General strung his troops thinly over a long front.

Doesn't Focus Thwart Creativity?

Some skeptics question the need for focus at all, and can point to examples where having no focus actually worked. But these examples are limited and anecdotal. The hard research evidence proves otherwise: A focused approach for new product development has been found to be an important ingredient of successful innovation strategies.[1] Focus provides direction for idea generation, criteria for idea screening and project selection, and targets for resource acquisition (Exhibit 3.1).

A second criticism is that focus inhibits creativity: Some of the best ideas may lie outside your targeted Strategic Arenas, and could be rejected as being "off strategy". The counter-argument is that focus improves creativity by targeting energies on those areas where the payoff is likely to be the greatest.[2] Further, significant new product breakthroughs outside

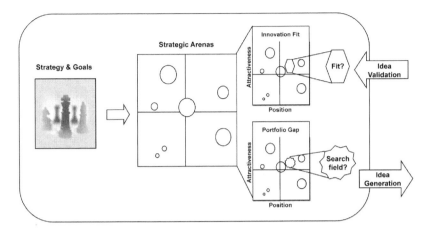

EXHIBIT 3.1: Strategy development entails the selection of strategic arenas – where you wish to focus your R&D and NPD efforts. Arenas are vital for idea generation (they provide the "search fields") and idea validation (idea screening: fit with the strategy).

the bounds of your new product strategy can usually be readily accommodated in an ongoing project screening process (which allows a certain percentage of outlier or off-strategy projects), or via free time or scouting projects. Inevitably there will be products that "got away" in any new product effort. But ample opportunities will continue to exist within the defined arenas for your business to exploit, provided you do a credible job of defining and selecting the strategically best areas to focus on.

Three Steps to Choosing Arenas

Defining target arenas answers the question: On what business, product, market, or technology areas should your business focus its new product efforts? Perhaps equally important, they define what areas are out-of-bounds or off-limits – areas that you should not enter with new products (Exhibit 3.2).

There are three steps to defining the target Strategic Arenas:

1. The first is strategic analysis – assessing your marketplace, technology and industry as well as your own company and its strengths (left box, Exhibit 3.3). This strategic analysis – the topic of this chapter – helps to identify potential strategic arenas and also provides insights into their relative attractiveness.
2. The second step is developing a comprehensive list of possible arenas – where you might focus your new product efforts.
3. The third is paring the list down – assessing the opportunities to yield a choice of the target arenas for you. Steps two and three are the topics of the next chapter.

Then, once the target arenas are selected, you move to defining attack plans, identifying specific new product opportunities, and executing selected development programs (right box, Exhibit 3.3).

- **A strategy statement that specifies those areas...**
  - Where development is to proceed
  - Identifies those areas that are off-limits

- **Defining the target arenas answers the question:**
  - On what business, product, market, or technology should the business focus its new product efforts?

The Task

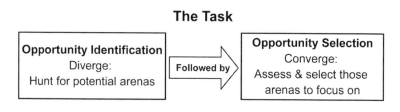

EXHIBIT 3.2: Target arenas must be defined for your business as part of your product innovation strategy.

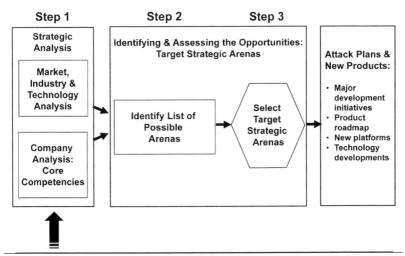

EXHIBIT 3.3: The three major steps to defining your Arenas of strategic focus begin with a solid strategic analysis – a hard look at your external environment (market and industry) and at your own company – its strengths and core competencies.

STEP 1: Strategic Analysis: Your Market, Technology and Industry

Here the purpose is to identify possible profitable, emerging, growing or interesting arenas – markets, market segments, technologies and product classes or categories – which might become candidate target arenas for you to focus your innovation efforts on. This strategic analysis should not only identify possible arenas on which your business might focus, it should also provide the quality data so important to evaluating and selecting the arenas that are right for your company. Key actions include assessment of your external environment; namely, your industry and market. Here are some valuable approaches:

Develop a Map of Your Value Chain

Map your value chain, identifying the key players. Your value chain includes your suppliers, as well as your customers, and their customers, right down to the ultimate user. Assess the futures of all the different members of this value chain, and their possible changing roles. Key questions include:

- Who are the players?
- What are their roles?
- Are these roles changing?
- Who is gaining and who is losing?
- Who controls your value chain?
- Who might be dis-intermediated (cut out)? And why?
- What changes are occurring in your value chain?
- How will the changes affect your industry and its key players?

Do the answers to these questions reveal any new opportunities, "aha's" and strategic moves you might consider? For example, what new opportunities could emerge from new value chains, or from changes in your existing value chain? And are there opportunities to capitalize on your changing environment?

Example: A major manufacturer of high-end synthetic kitchen countertops undertook an analysis of its downstream value chain. Numerous players are involved in the installation of countertops: the manufacturer, the fabrication shop, the kitchen designer, the retailer and the installer. To its surprise, the manufacturer discovered that the bulk of the profits was going to other members of the value chain. For example, the fabricator not only cuts the countertop to size, but often adds edging in the form of multiple layers, which is then machined to a contoured edge – a highly desired feature for high-end installations, but also very pricey. Strategically, the manufacturer made a commitment to get control of the distribution channel, obtain its fair share of the profit pool, and enter a new business by offering molded and contoured countertop products to move some of the fabricator value-add to the manufacturer. Imagine the lost opportunity had this company not undertaken to map its value chain.

Conduct an Industry Structure Analysis

Look at your industry structure, including your direct and indirect competitors. Often, analysis of competitors (their strategies, successes and failures) reveals insights into possible strategic moves you could make. Key questions include:

- Who are your major competitors – both direct and indirect (indirect: a competitor that is satisfying the same need as you, but with a different product or service)?
- Which competitor is winning and which is losing? Why?
- What are their strategies to get business?
- Which competitor is the most innovative? What are they up to?
- Have your competitors identified new or emerging customer needs that you may have missed? How are they satisfying them?
- Have any of your competitors identified new markets, segments or applications?
- Are they succeeding here (gaining sales and making money)? Why and how?
- Could you do a better job in these new arenas and win?

Do the answers to these questions point to any potential strategic opportunities for you – do they suggest any new areas, markets segments or product types that you should at least consider in your strategic exercise? And does this analysis suggest anything about the relative attractiveness of these new opportunities?

Identify Your Customers' Industry Drivers

Take a hard look at your customers and their industry. Assess what factors make your customers profitable and successful. Are these factors and drivers changing in a way that might open up opportunities for you? Are there opportunities for you to provide new solutions to help your customers?

> *Example:* A UK plastic bottle manufacturer was facing tough competition and declining margins with its traditional PET plastic bottles sold to the "squash" soft drinks market. (In the UK, a major category of soft drinks is not carbonated hence not pressurized. They are concentrated fruit flavored beverages called "squash"). The beverage companies, in turn, faced enormous price pressure from the four major retail chains in the UK, which are very powerful. An analysis of the retail firms' costs and profits in this drink category revealed that revenue per square foot of shelf space was vital, and that it was monitored very closely. Additionally, they discovered that the squash beverage firms were always desirous of differentiating their products on the shelf, hoping to de-commoditize their offerings in this near-commodity category.
>
> So the bottle manufacture came up with a new strategy of offering specially shaped PET bottles that could help their beverage customers solve their problems; maximizing revenue per square foot on the shelf while differentiating their products at point-of-purchase. First, the bottle manufacturer offered the novel concept of almost square soft drink bottles, so that more product could be placed on each square foot of shelf space. Because these beverages are not pressurized, the square bottle was technically feasible. By offering the option of custom-shaped bottles, the manufacturer helped the beverage company differentiate their otherwise bland products on the shelf. It was a win for both the beverage company and the retailer, and a definite win for the bottle manufacturer.

Show Me the Money!

Assess where the profits are to be found in your industry and in your value chain. Then ask why your business may be missing out on its fair share. For example, develop profit pool maps or market maps that illustrate who makes the money in your industry, market or value chain, as shown in Exhibit 3.4.[3]

> *Example:* A major North American financial institution (we'll call it ABC Bank) is reviewing its strategy for its commercial custody and trust business. (Custody and trust is the service whereby securities are held by a foreign bank on your behalf; for example, suppose an American purchases shares of a German company on the Frankfurt DAX stock exchange; the local German broker does not transfer the shares to you in the US, but rather holds them in a German bank in trust for you for a fee). The custody and trust business is a huge one for many international banks due to the amount of international trading in securities.
>
> Construction of the market map for this industry reveals some provocative findings for ABC Bank's executives. For example, in Exhibit 3.4, the custody and trust business is only 25 percent of the industry profits (center column) (ABC Bank is located in the centre column). More profitable but related sectors are services, such as, the transactions that must occur as a result of the securities purchase (almost 40 percent of the industry profits) and the settlement information that must flow back and forth between those parties involved in the transaction (settlement information, again almost 40 percent of industry profits). And a closer inspection of the centre column reveals that the traditional banking sector only accounts for about 20 percent of custody profits, with other institutions having a much larger share.
>
> This kind of chart reveals where profits are to be made. It is also a useful stimulus to help identify related, adjacent and profitable arenas, and the possibilities of targeting these. In the case of ABC Bank, the purchase of a trust company (center column) might be an option. Far

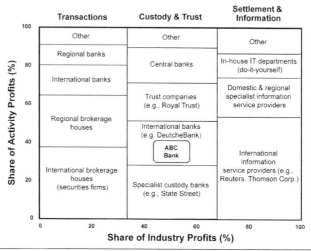

EXHIBIT 3.4: Market maps reveal the distribution of an industry's profits along two dimensions – industry function and type of company. The example here is the commercial custody and trust business (Financial Institutions).[3]

more interesting would be leveraging ABC Bank's superb international IT system to provide settlement information for its custody clients (a service that is currently offered by information firms such as Thompson Financial and Reuters, but not by ABC Bank).

Track Market Trends

Shifts and dislocations in markets offer opportunities to be exploited. So undertake a market and industry trend analysis: Examine historical trends and estimate future trends; and forecast market size and shifts. Next, measure market growth and volumes by segment, and identify qualitative trends that offer new opportunities. Look for possible disruptions in your industry and in your customers' industries. Finally, look for opportunities (or threats) that can be exploited and new markets, segments or potential arenas.

The point of this analysis is to seek niches or holes in the marketplace: areas that may be emerging, or may be underserved, or have been missed altogether.

Example: The trend to "better-for-you" and "wellness" was picked up early by the nutriceutical firm Meade-Johnson. The firm's market research also revealed that many menopausal females were facing problems when it came to nutrition: first, a lack of knowledge (many were confused about nutritional needs); and, second, a lack of key nutrients such as calcium and certain important vitamins due to on-the-fly eating habits. A third trend was identified: That many women in this age-group were simply tired – tired of working nine-to-five, and tired of talking care of their spouses and children. They needed to be indulged more.

The identification of the congruence of these trends led to a completely new arena for Meade-Johnson: nutriceutical wellness products aimed at this tired and in-need segment. The end result was a line of good-for-you products under the name Viactiv: indulgent snack products with the nutritional elements required by the age group. The first launch was calcium soft chews, a chewy chocolate laced with calcium and vitamin K for bones. Others included a power bar and a wine spritzer drink, equally indulgent but offering nutritional benefits. The line went on to become a huge success. It is now owned and marketed by McNeil Nutricionals, a division of Johnson & Johnson.

Check That the Five Forces Are Present

Whenever new niches or areas are identified that might offer potential, do a quick check into the relative attractiveness of this arena. A good model to use is the Five Forces model in Exhibit 3.5.[4] This model identifies five factors or forces that determine whether an arena will be profitable or not:

- *The strength of suppliers:* Beware of opportunities where the up-stream suppliers are very powerful and controlling. For example, the UK bottle manufacturer (above) must purchase PET polymers from large and powerful plastics firms as suppliers (although that supply market has become more competitive with the entry of low cost PET polymers from Asia).

- *The power of the customers:* Facing a handful of major and powerful customers is not an enviable position to be in. The bottle manufacture sells to a handful of major soft-drink beverage companies with very sharp purchasing departments.

- *The strength and intensity of competitors:* Highly competitive industries where the emphasis is on price competition generally led to lower margins and poor profits. The bottle manufacturer has a number of effective competitors in the UK and Europe with essentially the same technology and manufacturing processes.

- *The ease with which players can enter and exit:* Sectors where competitors can enter or exit relatively easily are less profitable; for example, where there are few technology, IP, or capital barriers. Here, the bottle manufacturer fares somewhat better: capital equipment and the technological know-how (extrusion blow molding) is somewhat difficult and expensive to acquire.

- *The threat of substitutes:* Whenever a market or sector is facing substitution threats, profits drop. The bottle manufacturer does

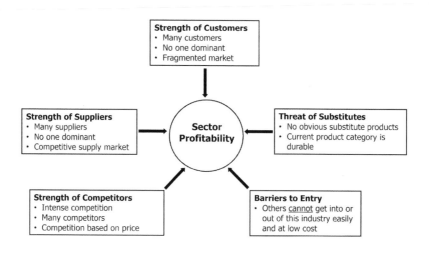

EXHIBIT 3.5: The Five Forces model shows the drivers of profitability in an industry sector, and helps to identify the really attractive arenas.[4]

indeed face threats of substitutes – from glass, other types of plastic, tetra-packs, paper-based containers, and other more environmentally friendly products.

All in all, the bottle manufacturer's business fails on four out of five forces, which explains why its margins and profits were in trouble – at least before its new shaped bottles initiative.

Spell out Different Scenarios of Your Market's Future

Most forecasts are wrong! Things simply don't turn out as expected – especially in business over this last decade. So it is somewhat surprising that, when painting a picture of the future, strategists usually assume that their forecasts are right and then base their strategies on these dubious forecasts.

When assessing your industry and market and its future, be sure to develop your "most probable estimate of the future". But don't stop there. Identify and forecast other possible futures. Include a worst-case scenario, or a most-unlikely case scenario. Then develop separate strategies based on these differing scenarios of the future, for example, different new products, or decisions to enter different arenas. This gives you options, just in case another view of the future actually does occur. Next, assign probabilities to each of your scenarios. Often, even a small probability that an unexpected case could arise will cause you to change your mind about possible new products to develop, new markets to target, or new technologies to acquire.

Finally, develop signposts that will signal which scenario of the several you have postulated is actually occurring. These signposts are important early warning signals, and are based on the premise that "what has not been foreseen is unlikely to be seen in time".

Examples:
- Most firms were caught off guard by the calamitous downturn in the economy in 2008-2009, in spite of the fact that there were

many economic indicators – from excessive personal debt to over-inflated housing prices – that signaled negative times ahead.

- Almost every company was surprised by the rapid adoption of the Internet and the profound changes it has had on the way business is conducted in almost every industry.

But there were signposts and signals that preceded these events and trends which could have been used as early warning signals. Here's a hypothetical example of scenario analysis, but based on a real-life case:

Example: A pet food manufacturer is engaged in strategy development and creates a multi-year forecast of the volume of the pet food market. The forecast is based largely on past trends, and the assumption that people will continue to have dogs and cats, and will continue to purchase pet food for them. Call this forecast "the official view of the future". Strategy is then developed based on this single forecast or official view, a strategy that includes new and improved pet food products, better packaging, and novelties such as pet snacks. Thus far, the strategic exercise is fairly traditional.

But wait! We know that this view of the future could well be wrong. For example, many forecasters are strong believers that demographics – the age distribution of the population – drive markets. And as demographic groups like Baby Boomers, Generation X and Y, and now the Net-Generation move through society, they have an enormous impact on markets. Baby Boomers have strongly influenced the housing market, the automotive market, the entertainment market, and just about every other market you can name during the last six decades.

Given that demographics drive everything, why not develop an alternate scenario of the future for pet food.

- *Question:* If Baby Boomers drive markets, what's happening to Baby Boomers?
- *Answer:* They're aging and reaching retirement, usually in good health and with financial assets.

- *Question*: What happens when you have a generation of people with cash, time on their hands, and good health?
- *Answer*: They travel abroad, and/or they winter in warm places.
- *Question*: What's the last thing people who travel want to own?
- *Answer*: Pets! They've loved their pets, but once the pet dies, it is not replaced.

Thus a new, "demographics-based scenario" for the pet food company is that traditional pet owners, from the Baby Boomer segment, will own far fewer pets in the future.

At first glance, this is a horrifying scenario for a pet food manufacturer; but it's also one that opens up new opportunities. The need is for "convenient pets" or "travel-friendly pets" which creates new product categories such as rent-a-pet services, automated pet feeders, pet hotels, travel pet foods, pet substitutes, and so on. There is a multitude of exciting services and products that are not food based that could certainly leverage the brand name, consumer trust and distribution system of this well-known pet food company.

As for signposts, this company currently tracks "pet ownership" statistics. But the key new metric becomes "pet acquisition by those over 60 years", a quite different and telling metric, and one that much better forecasts whether the "official view of the future" is really happening.

Undertake a Technology Forecast

Where is product technology heading in your industry? Be sure to undertake a technology assessment to determine the future of your industry's and products' technology. For example, what will be the performance of products based on that technology, and when? Commonly used methods of technology forecasting include the Delphi method, forecasts by analogy, and extrapolation of growth curves. Because disruptive technologies and radical or step-changes in technology performance are special cases of technology forecasting, we have reserved that discussion for the next section.

Delphi: The Delphi method is a systematic way to integrate the collective wisdom of a well-informed group of experts. The method can be used remotely or in a face-to-face meeting (modified Delphi or Estimate-Talk-Estimate). Carefully select technology experts from inside (and perhaps from outside) your company, and engage the group in a discussion on pre-specified questions about the future of the technology you are trying to forecast. At the end of the discussion, ask each person to write down their views on the various questions. Collect and display these views anonymously. Begin additional discussion, notably on the topic areas where there is disagreement. After several rounds, you will usually find there is consensus on the forecast. This method has proven to be a powerful and effective way to undertake forecasting, not only for technologies, but also for markets.

Growth curves: Most technology development follows a fairly predictable growth, or S-shaped, curve over its lifetime (Exhibit 4.8 in the next chapter). Axes are a metric that gauge performance (vertical) plotted against effort or time (horizontal).

What the growth or S-curves usually show is that, in the early days of a technology, progress is quite slow; then a tipping point is reached, and for many years much improvement in performance is made quickly. But as the technology matures, progress once again slows down as it becomes more difficult to make performance improvements. If you can plot the S-curve in your industry's technology, then it is usually possible to extrapolate the curve into the future and use this as a basis for technology forecasts.

Example: A producer of reverse-osmosis filtration equipment for municipal water purification plants witnesses fairly steady increases in the performance of these filters over the years. Technologists plot filter performance (liters per square meter per minute, for a given pressure differential) by years, and note an almost linear improvement in these filters – more water can be filtered by the same size filter. Extrapolating the curve shows what probably will be the performance of this technology in the years ahead; thus, what new products and what new applications will become technically (and economically) feasible.

Example: The well-known Moore's Law, which describes long-term trends in the history of computing hardware, is a special case of the technology S-curve. Since the invention of the integrated circuit in 1958, the number of transistors that can be placed inexpensively on an integrated circuit has increased exponentially, doubling approximately every two years.

Analogies: Often what takes place in technologies in other industries provides clues as to what might happen in your own industry. Plot the technology growth or S-curves of related or analogous technologies, look at their shapes and patterns, and then use this to forecast your own technology future.

Be a Head's Up Company

One senior executive of a major multinational company confessed that "We are a head's down company – much like a farmer trudging behind his plow, head down, carefully watching his plow." The executive went on, "Once in a while, we need to stop plowing, straighten up in the middle of the field, and have a darn good look around to see where we are, and where we're heading. But that's rare. We've got to become a heads up company!". So what kind of company are you – heads down, diligently following and watching the plow, or heads up? And how does one become more like a heads up company?

Don't Get Blind-Sided – Employ Peripheral Vision

Many companies are blind-sided by unexpected events.[5] First, these firms and their executives appear to be unaware of events and trends that come at them; yet these trends have the potential for doing damage or creating opportunities. In a strategic survey, two-thirds of companies were surprised by up to three high impact competitive events in the last five years; and, 97 percent of firms lack an early warning system.[6] Second, even if they do see trends coming, many firms appear unwilling or unable to take action – they're paralyzed like a deer in the headlights.

Example: Mattel, one of the world's largest toy makers and owner of the Barbie Doll brand, failed to recognize that pre-teen girls were maturing at younger ages – that they wanted to be more like their older sisters. Thus, they were outgrowing dolls like Barbie and shifting to more sophisticated dolls, such as Bratz. The shift drove down Barbie's sales dramatically after decades of prosperity, and appeared to catch the company sleeping. How could Mattel's' market research have missed this trend? Why were they blind-sided so badly? And if they saw it coming, why didn't they take action?

Example: DuPont invented many of the polymers that have become household names over the last 70 years: Nylon, Orlon, Dacron, Lycra, and Teflon. In time, patents expired and other firms began to compete in these markets. But DuPont's management failed to recognize and deal with a huge new threat of low cost polymers coming from Asia. Instead, DuPont made the ill-fated decision to retreat from their traditional polymers markets and products – which they created! This led to under-utilizing of production capacity, higher production costs and even greater vulnerability to lower cost products. A more viable strategy would have been to focus on those polymers where they had technological leadership and to leverage that technology position while, at the same time, building production capacity in Asia to achieve lower costs. This has been an effective strategy by many traditional US producers who find themselves in near-commodity and vulnerable businesses. Today DuPont struggles as it tries to reinvent itself – a far cry from the dominant technological and product innovative leader it once was.

The biggest dangers are the ones you don't see coming: Understanding these threats and anticipating the opportunities requires strong peripheral vision. Where Mattel failed, another toy firm had peripheral vision, and picked up on the fact that children were maturing faster.

Example: Throughout the 1990s, Lego's management in Denmark was well aware that little boys were growing up more quickly. They wanted to be like their older brothers, playing computer games on their PCs. For a building block maker like Lego, this could prove disastrous. Indeed, for a few years Lego saw sales and profits fall.

But beginning in the 1990s, Lego's management attempted to chart strategies and define new arenas where they could leverage their brand name, distribution and loyal customer base to advantage. A computer-based educational product line targeted at educators was attempted but did not do too well. Still, management did not give up. Then came the strategic breakthrough: robotics and electronics combined with Lego's modular brick concepts to produce Mindstorms, a huge success. Log onto Lego's webpage and look at their Mindstorms offering: imaginative, differentiated, exciting, a higher price point, fun for Dad too – it sure is a far cry from the Lego bricks most of us grew up with!

Lego has not stopped there. Their latest service-product is an online digital designer. This allows children to use online software (much like CAD) to design their own Lego toy – an airplane, or spaceship, or building. The software then reverse-engineers the design and creates a parts list, assembly instructions, and a box (the child can even design the box's cover). A price and delivery date are also displayed, so a parent can order the toy the child has just designed. Not only that, but the new toy product is now displayed to the Lego online community, so thousands of other kids can see and admire it. And of course, it becomes a standard item in Lego's product line. Besides getting customers to help design products, Lego's management now gains significant new insights into what their target customers really want. All of this reduces the chances of being blind-sided in the future!

Contrast the Lego story with Mattel's. Far from ignoring the threat, Lego's management dealt with reality and, after several not-so-successful attempts, flipped a serious threat into a great business opportunity. Peripheral vision and the willingness to act on it pays off!

The key peripheral vision questions: Here are the key questions you should address in your peripheral visioning exercise:[5]

- What are the major trends and events that are happening in your marketplace or industry? What is their impact: opportunity or threat? How big? Are you doing anything about them?
- Who in your industry picks up on advance warnings and acts on them? Surely some of your competitors seem to be ahead of the wave. Who are they, and what are they up to now?
- What have been your blind spots in the past? Have you missed trends and events? In what areas (markets, competitors, technology) and why?
- Is there a relevant analogy from another industry? For example, experiences in the genetically modified food business should provide useful insights for management in other new-and-controversial technology areas, such as nanotechnology.
- What are peripheral customers (customers in adjacent markets, and your former customers) and non-direct competitors saying?
- What new futures could really hurt (or help) you?
- Is there an unthinkable scenario of the future?

Assess the Potential Impact of Disruptive Technologies

Disruptive technologies have the potential to create major dislocations in an industry, often overnight, and frequently without much notice. And they can also create huge new opportunities – a new arena, a new business – for those who see them coming and take action. But disruptive technologies are often hard to predict, and their revenue impact is even harder to forecast. Thus, disruptive technologies present difficult challenges in terms of technology and industry trend analysis and strategy development.[7]

When disruptive technologies have occurred over the last century, in 90 percent of the cases, they have been missed or misread by the dominant firms in the industry: These incumbent firms grossly underestimated the impact of the new technology, and failed to develop a strategy to exploit it; thus they were no longer dominant after the new technology took hold. It's called the *tyranny of success:* What made firms successful in the first place then sows the seeds of defeat in the future.[8] They become complacent, set in their ways, and heavily invested in the old technologies and related operations (for example, in manufacturing facilities). And it is a worldwide dilemma; look at the evidence:

- The entire Swiss watch industry was all but devastated by digital watches almost overnight. The Swiss watch industry failed to develop an adequate strategy and sat on the sidelines as the digital time-keeping industry shifted to Japan.
- The electronic hand-held calculator destroyed the dominant calculator manufacturers – producers of slide-rules and adding machines – within a few years of its introduction. But none of the slide-rule makers shifted into electronics.
- The xerographic photocopier destroyed traditional copier machines like the Gestetner machine and Kodak's' office photographic process, as well carbon paper. The market was still there – office copies were still needed – but in a new and better way. Ironically, in spite of the fact that Kodak's and Xerox's headquarters were within a few miles of each other in Rochester, NY, and no doubt each was well aware of the other, Kodak never launched an adequate office copier product.
- The ball-point pen wiped out most fountain-pen manufactures in short order, leaving only a handful of high-end fountain-pen suppliers today.
- The digital camera caught major suppliers of traditional photography products by surprise. Two leading firms saw their sales plummet: Kodak's film business dropped dramatically and Polaroid went out of business altogether.

- The Internet with its interactive capability is rendering traditional one-way communication – such as that provided by the main-stream television networks – a thing of the past, as young people spend more time online than watching traditional TV.

The list goes on, but you get the point.

What is a disruptive technology? The great majority of new products are based on existing technologies; and the resulting new products usually result in improved performance and more customer benefits. This type of development work is often called "incremental innovation" or "sustaining innovation" (Exhibit 3.6) and occurs on an ongoing basis in most industries. For example, 35 mm cameras steadily improved decade-by-decade, largely through incremental innovation and product improvements. But the technology remained essentially the same: light-activated 35 mm film and a shutter-device camera. Over time, the performance may actually surpass what customers need or want – the dashed line in Exhibit 3.6. By the time digital cameras were introduced, more sophisticated 35 mm cameras boasted so many features and functionalities that the average consumer was overwhelmed.

Then comes the disruption: New products are developed based on a totally new technology as in the case of digital cameras. Ironically, these new products actually yield inferior performance compared to existing products based on the "old technology" when measured on traditional performance metrics (Exhibit 3.6). In fact, their performance is often well below what customers want or expect... at least in the beginning. But, over time, their performance steadily improves. For example, the first digital cameras were inferior in many ways to 35 mm. The picture quality was poor; the capacity to take multiple pictures was severely limited; and getting good prints was difficult. Today technology has improved to the point where digital cameras delight most customers.

The new "disruptive technology" products may perform badly on traditional metrics in the beginning, but the danger to incumbents is that they bring a new performance dimension or a new value proposition to the market (See the Z-dimension in Exhibit 3.6). Thus, while the

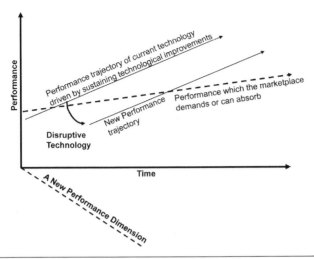

ExHIBIT 3.6: New products based on a disruptive technology initially under-
perform current-technology products. But the new technology adds a new
dimension (dashed line) that has value to a sub-segment of users.[7,8]

incumbent suppliers and the bulk of their customers are still thinking in
the two-dimensional plane of Exhibit 3.6 (where the traditional products
perform much better), the new entrants and their customers are really
operating in a three-dimensional world. A case in point: Although the
first digital cameras actually produced a lower resolution picture than
traditional 35 mm film cameras, the fact that the new technology yielded
a digitized picture was a real bonus for a handful of users. They saw real
benefits in being able to electronically transmit the photos. These users
included commercial real estate agents and property insurance adjusters:
They did not need award-winning pictures or even prints. The fact that
they could shoot and send the photo by email to head office or a client
offered real value - so much so that they were prepared to put up with the
disadvantages of the early digital cameras. Admittedly, these very early
adopters or "bleeding edge users" were tiny market segments, but they did
pave the way for subsequent improvements and eventual adoption of
digital cameras by the mainstream market. The early PC market emerged
in much the same way.

They come at you stealthily: Disruptive technologies are doubly dangerous to incumbent firms, partly because they pose a real threat to current products, but also because they are often very stealthy. The inferior performance is what makes the impact and timing of disruptive technologies so hard to predict. In the beginning the industry experts, product pundits, forecasters and market researchers conclude that the new product based on the new technology is clearly inferior, and that it will never catch on. That was the initial reaction of Polaroid executives, who pushed ahead aggressively with traditional Polaroid camera development. Kodak executives were more aware of the digital threat to their traditional business, but they underestimated how fast and how strong it would come. Thus, the fact that the disruptive technology comes quietly and tends to be dismissed by many experts is what makes it so threatening. By the time you see it coming, it's too late to take action.

One problem with the theory is that it is difficult to predict the success and timing of disruptive technologies. This leads some critics to charge that disruptive technology theory explains history very well, but it is not very useful for forecasting the future. For example, the cell phone, when first introduced, displayed all the characteristics of a disruptive technology. It had inferior initial performance; size and weight (using an early cell phone was like speaking into a brick); and limited battery life (so much so that car phones with ready access to power were the only practical applications initially). But cell phones added a new value or dimension – portability – which had appeal to some users such as business people on the move who spent a lot of time in a car. So cell phones gained market momentum. This led to subsequent improvements to the point where today many users no longer even maintain "land lines".

By contrast, a similar product – the satellite phone – had many of the same classic characteristics of a disruptive technology, but it suffered a very different fate. This satellite phone technology enabled users to communicate with a hand-held phone directly via satellite, and eliminated dead-zones and the need for cell towers. Many pundits predicted it would obsolete the cell phone. But for the end-user, there were few benefits. Most consumers already received adequate cell phone reception, while the size and bulk of satellite phones, coupled with a one-second time lag, were strong enough negatives to kill the product for mainstream use (although satellite phones are still used in remote areas, such as in the arctic or a board ocean ships). But who could have predicted cell phones to be a big winner, and satellite phones to be the loser – except in hindsight?

Look for the advance signals: The point is that you cannot afford to dismiss disruptive technologies, simply because the initial products offer poor performance. Many of the hundreds of major firms that made this mistake are no longer in business. Rather, treat the new technology as an opportunity that should be monitored and investigated. Be sure to identify potential disruptive technologies and radical or step-change innovations as part of your industry analysis. Assess the probability and timing of each, the potential impact, and whether or not it represents an opportunity (or a threat) for your business. And, most importantly, ask "so what?" – what can and should you do about this technology? Here are six tips for assessing and forecasting disruptive technologies in your industry:

1. Continually monitor the outside technology landscape in your own industry:
   - Identify technologies that might address your current customers' drivers better than your own technology does.
   - Monitor the technologies in those industries working on related problems.
2. Understand the dynamics of innovation and substitution. There are reasons why new technologies emerge:
   - An unmet customer need that the current technology cannot meet.
   - A new customer need as a result of shifts in the external environment.
3. Understand the causes and assess whether the new technology is likely to satisfy that need:
   - In planning to anticipate disruptive technologies, don't start with the technology, but begin with customer needs.
   - Understand what the customer or user sees as having value.

4. Look beyond what customers ask for – look to their real needs and benefits sought, not just their wants.
5. Look beyond the mainstream market:
   - Identify the handful of potential customers who stand to benefit the most from the new solution.
   - Focus on sub-segments in the market place – the very early adopters.
6. Do field work:
   - Hold face-to-face discussions with these early adopters.
   - Learn first-hand about applications and users' potential for adoption.

Complete Your IOTA Analysis

Now it's time to integrate all your conclusions about what's happening in your industry and markets that could open new opportunities or pose threats. In this summary, create an "impact table" or chart, using the template in Exhibit 3.7 as a guide. This is called an IOTA chart (short for Impact of Opportunity and Threats Analysis). This chart looks a lot like an FMEA (Failure Modes Effects Analysis, used in product design), except that it is strategic in nature and for your entire business.

The fundamental questions of this impact analysis are:

1. What are the major threats, significant changes and trends, disruptions, danger signals, key issues and events taking place in your industry and market? List these.

   Note that topic areas are provided down the left side of the chart as prompts (Exhibit 3.7) and include markets and customers, competitors, members of your value chain, technology, legal and regulatory, social and demographic, and economic trends.
2. How likely is the threat, change or event? Is it almost a certainty, such as an impending regulatory change, or a demographic reality; or, is it a "maybe" and highly uncertain, such as the emergence of a new technology?

3. What is the timing? Is it here and now, imminent within a year or two, or far off in the future?

4. What is the impact on your industry, market, and especially on your business? Is this an opportunity or a threat? If an opportunity, how big – what's the size of the prize here? And if a threat, what impact – will it devastate your business if you do nothing (as the growing-up-early phenomenon did to Mattel, and almost did to Lego)? Or will the change, threat or disruption have only a minor impact on your business?

5. Finally, what opportunities emerge from your analysis? What new business areas or strategic arenas, new markets, new product classes or new business models does your strategic analysis point to? This is perhaps the most important question, and requires some creativity and insight: the ability to translate trends, events, threats and disruptions into opportunities.

Area or Topic	What threats, major changes & trends, disruptions, and events are taking place in your market, industry & technology	How likely?	How imminent (timing)?	Impact on your business – opportunity or threat?	What opportunities: new arenas, product classes, new markets or new business models?
Market changes and shifts – your customers					
Changes in your competitors and their strategies					
Changes in members of your value chain (e.g. retailers, dealers)					
Technology changes and disruptions					
Legislative & political changes, events, dangers					
Social & demographic trends, changes					
Economic changes, threats, dangers					

EXHIBIT 3.7: Undertake an IOTA – Impact of Opportunities and Threats Analysis – in order to identify opportunities and new potential arenas.

Clearly the IOTA questions cover a broader area than one person can handle and some are particularly profound, such as the question in point number 5. Further, seeking robust answers requires much work, thought and insight. Thus, this facet of the analysis is best handled by a senior cross-functional group – likely the executive or leadership team of your business, supported by the people who have pulled the data and the analysis together. This is most definitely a place where a dozen heads and sets of eyes are better than one!

Leverage Your Core Competencies

Attack from a position of strength! Thus, a critical component of strategic analysis is an internal assessment, namely looking at your own business, trying to identify your unique strengths that can be leveraged to advantage. Many studies repeat the message: Leveraging your strengths and core competencies increases success rates and new product profitability.[9]

Many strategists misunderstand the concept of a core competency, and think that it is simply a strength. Not so. A company's core competency is defined as something it can do better than its competitors. But more: A core competency is critical to enabling the firm to create new products and services and to achieving competitive advantage with these products.

A core competency has three characteristics:[10]

1. It should make a significant contribution to the perceived customer benefits.
2. It can be leveraged widely to many products and markets.
3. It should be difficult for competitors to imitate.

A core competency can take various forms, including technical and IP know-how, a reliable manufacturing process, or close relationships with customers and suppliers. It may also include an effective product development capability or culture.

The point of undertaking a core competency assessment is to help you identify adjacencies (adjacent markets, sectors, and product classes) which you can attack from a position of strength. These adjacencies become potential new strategic arenas for your business. Leveraging your core competencies in new and adjacent arenas enables your business to create new products and services but, most importantly, it helps you achieve competitive advantage.

Example: A manufacturer of fuel lines for the automotive industry faced bleak markets and sought to define new arenas outside its current market. As part of its strategic exercise, management undertook a detailed core competency assessment. Many predicable core competencies and strengths were identified, such as their proficient production process in pipe manufacturing and their strong relationships with major automotive companies. But the breakthrough came when a technological skill was identified – namely in quick-connect fittings. The firm had invented the quick-connect fitting for use on its fuel lines to enable faster assembly on the automotive production line. This is a fitting that is a pull-tab plastic connection rather than a welded, soldered or threaded connection, which is much faster and easier.

When management moved to the next step of the strategic exercise, identifying potential arenas where each competency could be leveraged to advantage, they brainstormed. Where could they use this unique quick-connect fitting technology? One arena they identified was plumbing fixtures for the do-it-yourself market (have you ever tried to install a new faucet or plumbing fixture in your bathroom or kitchen? It's a knuckle-busting job). The firm hunted for a potential partner in the plumbing field, found a leading firm that was willing, and together they developed and produced the new line of do-it-yourself plumbing fixtures that doesn't need a wrench to install!

This plumbing business opportunity was but one of several new and adjacent arenas the company identified and pursued. The point is, were it not for a solid core competency assessment, this company probably would still be focused on the automotive sector, trying to eke out a living in a declining market with low margins.

Take a hard look at your business and undertake a core competencies assessment. Look at leveragable strengths in all facets of your business, and relative to your competitors:

- Your technology strengths, notably product and development technologies
- Your marketing, distribution, brand name and sales force strength
- Your operations or production capabilities, capacities and technology.

Assess your business on each item, especially relative to your direct and indirect competitors. Use the list of items in Exhibit 3.8 as a guide. Then identify areas where you are better than the rest: your core competencies.

---

1. **Your marketing competencies versus competitors' – your...**
   - Loyalty of key customer groups and your customer relationships
   - Brand name and reputation in the marketplace
   - Product – quality, performance, reliability, and value reputation
   - Distribution and channels (access to key customer groups)
   - Sales force (coverage, skills, reputation)
   - Advertising, communications and public relations skills
   - Service, support, and technical service skills
   - Market shares, presence in certain markets or segments, and reputation overall

2. **Your products and their technology versus competitors' – your...**
   - Areas of product leadership, technologically (features, functionality, product performance)
   - Development technology capabilities
   - Access to new technologies internally or externally
   - Unique technologies or technological skills
   - Intellectual property (IP) and proprietary positions

3. **Your operations capabilities, capacities, and technology versus competitors' – your...**
   - Production or operations resources, facilities and capacities
   - Unique skills or abilities (costs, volumes, flexibility, reliability)
   - Technological capabilities in production or operations
   - Unique production technologies, intellectual property, and protection
   - Unique access to raw materials
   - Workforce – their skills, knowledge, and availability

Exhibit 3.8: Assess your business's core competencies, using the rating items in this chart as a guide.

These are your unique and leveragable strengths, so you can now look for target arenas where you can leverage these strengths to advantage in the development of new products.

Strategic Assessment – Wrap-Up

Good strategists have many good options. Bad strategists find themselves in a box with few options and often no way out. Too often, managements begin this strategic exercise with blinders on – with a closed mind about what options they have and about which areas they can and will focus on. Not surprisingly, they arrive at a strategy that looks very much like their current one, and the results are predicable – no real improvement. A solid and insightful strategic analysis helps take the blinders off and opens your executive team's eyes to potential Strategic Arenas that they may not have seen or considered. Make no mistake: This type of an analysis is tough work. It requires discipline, and may take many hands to do well. But the effort is well worth it. Good strategic assessment is the key to "aha" moments and opportunities for new products that you, otherwise, would have missed.

Strategic Arenas – The Right Approach

It is more important to know where you are going than to get there quickly. Do not mistake activity for achievement.

Mabel Newcomber, 1892–1983

The Hunt for Strategic Arenas

The specification of your target Strategic Arenas provides an important guide to your product innovation efforts: "What is needed is a strategy statement that specifies those areas where development is to proceed and identifies (perhaps by exclusion) those areas that are off limits.".[1] Your target arenas provide direction for resource commitment and deployment. They guide the search for new product ideas and help in idea screening and project selection. Finally, delineation of where your business wishes to focus its new product efforts is critical to long-term planning, particularly for resource and skills acquisition. Without Strategic Arenas clearly defined, you have no focus (or the wrong focus) in your product innovation efforts.

This chapter moves from the strategic analysis of Chapter 3 into how to define a Strategic Arena, and then how to go about evaluating and selecting which one or ones are the best for you to focus on.

Too Close to Home?

When seeking focus, a major shortcoming is the failure to pick the "strategically winning arenas". Often the best Strategic Arenas lie a little farther from home, or may require a bit of a stretch for the business – they are more innovative and venturesome. Instead, senior management opts for the "low-hanging fruit" strategy or easy, comfortable strategy. While low-hanging fruit may be easy to pick, it is not always the tastiest. In short, the big danger here is the strong tendency to stay too close to home and, as a result, end up with strategies that lack much in the way of a bold or new thrust. Thus, many companies undertake a strategic exercise, but end up with a rather "ho hum" and defensive strategy – defend the base, or a strategy that says "do what we're now doing, only better."

Example: "We followed your model for developing an innovation strategy," a R&D executive in one business unit told us. "We identified potential Strategic Arenas, analyzed each, and then picked our best bets to focus on. The problem was: we just 'sliced and diced' our current business and markets a little more finely – more granular segmentation – and as a result, we ended up focusing on the areas that we're already in. We just can't seem to move out of the box we're in".

Clearly there is a time and place for a "defend the base" strategy, and the recommendation is certainly not that everyone should venture away from home-base when developing an innovation strategy. But think about the Apple and P&G cosmetics examples in Chapter 1: How management identified bold new strategic arenas to focus on – arenas that were adjacent to their current business, could leverage the companies' core competencies and strengths, but at the same time, were relatively new or emerging arenas to both firms (MP3 players for Apple; and for P&G, cosmetics to make women look younger).

An innovation strategy by definition requires you to be somewhat innovative and entrepreneurial – and that may mean putting your toes into new waters, or landing on new beachheads. So be it! Again, recall from Chapter 1 that one of the four themes that leads to success in innovation is having an offensive strategy (as opposed to strictly defensive) – a strategy that sees you attacking new arenas and striving to gain a position rather than simply defending a position. An offensive strategy focused on new arenas is not for everyone, but do keep this offensive thrust in the top-of-mind as you decide on arenas to focus on.

A useful chart to visualize where you wish to focus your new product efforts is in Exhibit 4.1. Here, the axes are technology newness to the company (how new or unfamiliar is this technology to you) and market newness to the firm (how new and unfamiliar is this market?). Arenas or clusters of arenas can be shown on this map; the most step-out, boldest and potentially the riskiest are in the upper right corner of Exhibit 4.1. A good strategist will seek a balance of arenas in terms of newness.

Example: Corning is a leading innovator in the glass business. Visit the company's museum in Corning, NY and see the history of their development of glass. Corning invented Pyrex, the catalytic converter and even fiber optics. But with the collapse of the fiber optic market in the high-tech crash of 2000, Corning's sales dropped to less than half, and share prices plummeted from $110 to just over one dollar almost overnight.[2] New technological and market opportunities were identified where the company could leverage its capabilities to advantage. But note, in mapping these new options, management did not just look to the current business, nor just to immediate and adjacent market arenas. Rather they employed the map in Exhibit 4.1 to plan a bold strategy that involved a reasonable balance of product and business extensions, but also new markets (market adjacencies) and, finally, totally new arenas and opportunities (new technology and new markets to the company).

By 2007, major innovations had been created for each business unit: four new business platforms and three major market adjacencies. New product sales rose to 70 percent of revenues, and Corning's profits soared from a loss of $500 million to a plus position of over $2 billion.

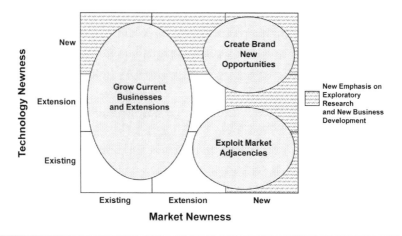

ExHIBIT 4.1: This Technology-Market newness chart helps you visualize the types of arenas you might wish to focus your R&D efforts on. In Corning's case, the shaded area shows the new areas of emphasis.[2]

But What Is a New Product Arena?

How does one define a Strategic Business Arena? We define Strategic Arenas as one of, or a combination of, a product category, product class, market, segment, industry sector, technology or manufacturing process on which a business decides to strategically focus its innovation resources. In this book, we sometimes refer to Strategic Arenas as "areas of focus", or "target arenas". A company might pick one Strategic Arena, or a number of them, as part of its innovation strategy. By selecting Strategic Arenas, a business can more readily focus its limited resources to effectively target promising opportunities.

There are many different ways that one can think about and define arenas, hence you need to be flexible in approaching the challenge, and selecting the approach that works for you. Here are some examples.

The product-market matrix: The product-market matrix is one way to visualize and identify strategic arenas. Here you construct a two-dimensional matrix, with the dimensions labeled "products" and "markets" in order to identify new business arenas, as in Exhibits 4.2 and

4.3.[3] The "markets" dimension includes your current and related or adjacent markets. And "products" includes your current as well as related and adjacent product types; for example, similar products to your current ones, or products that could be made in your existing production facilities, or developed using familiar and in-house technology. Each cell in the matrix represents a set of products that could be developed in response to needs in these markets. The cells thus define the opportunities for exploitation: the possible Strategic Arenas.

Example: Recall last chapter's example of the automotive fuel-pipe manufacturer facing a declining market. The core competency assessment revealed quick-connect fitting technology as a unique competency. Management then brainstormed about where such a technology might be employed. A number of possible markets and applications were identified (Exhibit 4.2). These included plumbing, appliances, computers and medical equipment. Besides connector products, the company also produces tubes, assemblies and molded plastic products. The resulting matrix of products and markets yields specific potential arenas where management might focus its product innovation efforts.

		New But Related Markets							
		Appliances	Spa/ Whirlpool	Plumbing	Natural Gas	Power Generation	Computers	Offshore	Medical
Product Types	Connector Products	Quick-connect inlet hoses	Quick-connect fittings	Quick-connect fixtures	Quick-connect fittings		Quick-connect cooling pipes		Quick-connect fittings
	Tube Products	Plastic/metal tubes	Plastic tubes	Plastic tubes		CuBe Tube	Plastic tubes	CuBe Tube	Plastic tubes
	Plastic Molded Products								
	Assemblies/ Systems	Assemblies	Bundles				Cooling systems		

EXHIBIT 4.2: The pipe manufacturer uses the product market matrix to identify potential areas in adjacent markets. On the left are the product types, and across the top the markets. Each cell represents a new area with many potential new products.

Several of these, including plumbing products, were selected, which led to the big success in do-it-yourself plumbing fixtures.

Example: Telenor, the main Norwegian telephone company, uses a product-market matrix to help visualize strategic choices and to define arenas on which to focus its new product efforts. One dimension of the matrix is "markets": SoHo (small office, home office), Business, Residential, the left side of Exhibit 4.3. The other dimension is the "products": (voice, data, Internet, wireless) across the top. The 10 by 10 matrix (not fully shown) identifies 100 cells, each a possible arena. Some can be ruled out immediately as not feasible. The remaining cells are evaluated, and priorities are established. The top priority arenas are singled out for intensive product development efforts.

Customer groups, functions and technologies: The product-market matrix approach can be taken one step farther by defining a business or strategic arena in terms of three dimensions:[4]

		Products		
		Voice	Data	Internet
	SoHo	✓		✓
	Medium Business			✓
Markets	Large Business		✓	✓
	Multinational		✓	
	Residential	✓		

- The axes of the diagram are 'Products' and 'Markets'
  - Products the company now sells, or related/adjacent products
  - Markets the company now serves or related/adjacent markets
- Each cell represents a potential strategic arena
- Arenas are assessed for their potential and the company's business position
- Check marks designate top priority arenas – where product innovation efforts will be focused

EXHIBIT 4.3: The product-market matrix is used by a telephone company to identify potential areas where it may focus its service-product development.

1. *Customer groups served:* For a computer manufacturer, customer groups include banks, manufacturers, universities, hospitals, retailers, etc.
2. *Customer functions served:* These include hardware applications, support and services, software, data storage, etc.
3. *Technologies utilized:* For data storage, several existing and new technologies might have application.

The result is a three-dimensional diagram, with new product arenas defined in this three-dimensional space.

Crawford's typology: A study of innovation charters points to several ways in which managers define new product arenas in practice.[5] Arenas are specified by (illustrations are for an industrial pump manufacturer):

- Product-type (for example, high pressure industrial pumps)
- End-user activity (chemical processors; or distributors)
- Type of technology employed (reciprocating; centrifugal; magneto-hydrodynamic)
- End-user group (oil refineries; polymers companies).

On its own, each of these arena definition schemes has its problems. For example, a product-type definition is limiting: Product-classes or product-types die. Similarly, an end-user group definition could lead your business into a number of unrelated technologies, products, and production systems.

The "who, what, how" method: A review of these and other methods for defining a business arena reveals that a single-dimension approach is often too narrow. However, a two- or three-dimensional approach, variants of the methods above, probably will suit most business contexts.[6] For example, define your product innovation arenas in terms of:

1. *Who:* the customer group to be served (markets or market segments)
2. *What:* the application (or customer need to be satisfied)

3. How: the technology required to design, develop, and produce products for the arena.

These three dimensions – who, what, and how – provide a useful starting point to describe New Product Arenas. Sometimes, the last two dimensions – what and how – can be simply combined into a single dimension, product type, which takes one back to the familiar product-market matrix above.

Popular dimensions used in industry: Often the simplest scheme is the best. Here are ways that we most often see management using in order to visualize strategic arenas:

- Customer groups (markets, segments)
- Industry sectors
- Product categories (for consumer goods) or product classes or types
- Customer functions (what function the customer performs, e.g. fabricators, processors, distributors)
- Technologies required to deliver solutions.

Selecting the Arenas: A Blow-by-Blow Illustration

Let's look more closely at some of the details of this process of searching for and prioritizing arenas. For this illustration, we use a real company, Chempro, a medium-sized manufacturer of process equipment (agitators and blenders) for the pulp and paper industry[1]. A two- or three-dimensional diagram can be used for this search and evaluation. You might also use the product-market matrix as in Exhibits 4.2 or 4.3, or any other convenient dimensions that define arenas for your business.

---

1. A real company, but some details have been disguised.

Defining Strategic Arenas at Chempro

The Chempro illustration: The company's major strength is its ability to design and manufacture rotary hydraulic equipment, and it is so focused technically that it has turned this rather narrow agitator-design "art" into a science. The market served is the pulp and paper industry; the application is agitation and blending of liquids and slurries.

Chempro's management elects the "who, what, how" approach above, namely the three dimensions of customer groups, applications, and technologies; these are shown as the X, Y, and Z axes of the diagram in Exhibit 4.4. Home-base or the current business is located, and then other opportunities are identified by moving away from home-base along each axis to other (but related) customer groups, applications, and technologies – to new but adjacent areas.

What New Product Arenas exist for the company? Clearly, the home-base is one of these, and indeed the firm is active in seeking new product ideas for agitation equipment in the pulp and paper field. Most of these opportunities, however, are limited to modifications and improvements, and the market is somewhat stagnant.

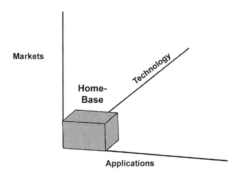

- 'Home-Base' is current markets, current technologies, current applications
- Move away from home-base in any direction and identify adjacencies

EXHIBIT 4.4: The "who, what, how" three-dimensional map is used in the Chempro example to define potential strategic arenas.

One direction that senior management can take is to develop new products aimed at related but new customer groups. These customer groups include the chemical, food-processing, petroleum-refining, and hydro-metallurgical fields. The options are shown across the top of the matrix in Exhibit 4.5.

Similarly, new products in related applications can be sought. These related applications include the pumping of fluids, fluid aeration, and refining and grinding, as shown on the vertical axis of Exhibit 4.5.

Considering these two dimensions – different applications and different customer groups – management now proceeds to define a number of new arenas. Working with the resulting two-dimensional matrix (Exhibit 4.5), recognize that, besides the home-base arena, there are 12 other arenas that the company can consider for its new product focus. For example, Chempro can develop blending and agitation equipment (same application) aimed at the chemical or petroleum industries (new customer groups). Alternatively, the business can develop aeration devices (new application) targeted at its current customers,

Adjacent Markets

		Pulp and Paper (home-base)	Chemical Process Industry	Petroleum Refining	Hydro-Metallurgical
Products that Build on Current Technology	**Agitation and Blending**	Home-Base: Agitators and blender for P&P industry	Chemical mixers and blenders	Blenders for petroleum storage tanks	Hydro-metallurgical mixers, agitators
	Aeration	Surface aerators for P&P: waste treatment	Aerators for chemical waste treatment plants	Aerators for chemical waste treatment plants	Aerators for floatation cells
	Wet Refining and Grinding	Pulper, repulpers and refiners			Wet refining equipment
	Specialty Plumbing	High density paper stock pumps	Specialty chemical pumps	Specialty petroleum pumps	Slurry pumps

EXHIBIT 4.5: Chempro management uses a two-dimensional matrix to denote possible strategic areas.

namely pulp and paper companies. Each of these possibilities represents a new arena for Chempro.

Chempro can move on the third dimension in Exhibit 4.4 by shifting from its home-base of rotary hydraulic technology to other technologies. If the technology options are superimposed along the third dimension, the result is a much larger number of possible arenas. Possible alternative arenas along the "new technologies" axis include magneto-hydrodynamic pumps and agitators for a variety of end-user groups; bio-oxidation for the food industry or waste treatment; and many others. (Note: This third dimension expansion is not shown in the matrix).

Selecting the Right Arenas

The task now is to narrow down the many possible arenas to a set that will become the focus of the business's innovation strategy. To a certain extent, a pre-screening of these arenas has already occurred; each has been identified as being adjacent or related to the base business on at least one of the three dimensions.

Now, the long list of arenas is narrowed to a shorter list by subjecting them to three knock-out questions to remove any of the non-starters:

1. Is this arena within the strategic mandate or vision of the company? Or is it so far off-base that, even with some imagination and an adjusted strategy, it would be way out of bounds? Try to keep an open mind on this knock-out question; otherwise you'll end up back in your own backyard with your current "same as" strategy.

   Example: An Irish beer company was identifying potential strategic arenas on which to focus its product innovation. Fairly standard arenas were identified – market segments such as "the female drinker who doesn't drink our brand" and the "metro-sexual male drinker who is particularly sensitive to his female partner's wishes". Packaging innovations was also an arena. But one arena proved simply to be too far off-base: the concept of franchising Irish Pubs, much like

McDonalds or Burger King. After all, the company has a globally recognized brand name that's almost synonymous with Irish pubs; and a sister company owned by the same parent at the time was in the franchising business (Burger King), so why not? After some discussion, this arena was deemed just too far off-base for this beer company. Other managements might have had a different opinion, although Diageo, the parent, has since sold Burger King to focus more on the alcoholic beverage business.

2. Is this arena really feasible, and is it feasible by your business (perhaps with some external help from partners)? Or is it simply too big an arena, or too much of a stretch for your business?

   Example: One ITT business identified "processing weak radio signals in an innovative way" as a core competency. The business unit makes GPS satellites and obviously has much experience in creating and handling weak signals from space, and with very limited electrical power supply. An obvious application of this capability is cell phones – replacing the rather high-powered and often ineffective radio signal transmission tower with far more clever systems, thereby improving reception and cutting power costs dramatically. This arena actually made it to a fairly short list, but finally was rejected as "being just too big for us to handle or do".

3. Does this arena fit with the company's values, ethics and philosophies? Often companies have ethics or philosophical statements that rule out certain types of businesses.

Those arenas that survive these knock-out questions comprise the "short list". Often there is further compression, as some arenas are so close to others that they are conveniently combined.

The Two Critical Strategic Dimensions

The choice of the right arenas boils down to how each one rates on two key dimensions or criteria. These are proven predictors of strategic success in product innovation, and have been identified in our studies of successful new product strategies. They are: "Arena Attractiveness" and "Business Strength", as defined in Exhibit 4.6.

1. Arena Attractiveness: This strategic dimension is externally oriented, and captures how attractive the external opportunities are within that arena. Is this Strategic Arena lush and fertile with ample opportunities for profitable new products? Or is it sterile offering few opportunities for innovation and growth? This dimension consists of:

- *Market attractiveness:* the size, growth, and potential of market opportunities within the arena; and,
- *Technological opportunities:* the degree to which technological and new product opportunities exist within the arena.

The Two Key Strategic Dimensions

1. **Arena Attractiveness**
    - How attractive are the opportunities in this arena?
      - A. Market attractiveness
      - B. Technological opportunities
    - An external measure
2. **Business Strength**
    - What do you bring to the table to suggest that you'll be an effective competitor in this arena?
    - Your relevant strengths and position
    - Can you leverage your Core Competencies to advantage here?
    - An internal measure

Rate each potential strategic arena on both dimensions

EXHIBIT 4.6: Two key strategic dimensions are used to rate the potential arenas. Both are drivers of success in product innovation.

In practice, Arena Attractiveness is a composite index constructed by rating the arena on a number of detailed criteria that capture market growth, size and the potential for new products. A typical list of these criteria is shown in Exhibit 4.7. You should adapt this list to suit your own business and industry. After you rate each arena based on these criteria, the scores can be added to yield an Index of Arena Attractiveness. Arenas that feature large, growing and high-potential markets that are characterized by technological elasticity (dynamic technologies, and many new product introductions) score high on the Arena Attractiveness dimension.

One criterion in Exhibit 4.7 that gauges technological opportunities – the potential for developing new products – is technological elasticity. The technology S-curve in Exhibit 4.8 helps you to assess how these arenas are likely to fare. Technological elasticity is the slope of the technology S-curve: the curve that plots product performance, versus

Arena Attractiveness

A. Market attractiveness
  - Size of the markets in this arena (dollar volume)
  - Number of potential customers for the product in this arena
  - Market growth rates
  - Competitive intensity and strength (negative)
  - Margins earned by others here
  - Long term potential of markets in this arena

B. Technological opportunities
  - Rate of change of technology in this arena (mature, stagnant = poor)
  - Introduction rate of new products in this arena (few, stagnant = poor)
  - Technological elasticity:
    - Opportunity for developing new products in this arena
    - Will a dollar spent yield significant performance improvements in future new products?

Rate your potential Arenas on these questions.
This becomes the vertical axis on the Strat-Map (Exhibit 4.10)

EXHIBIT 4.7: Dimension 1 is 'Arena Attractiveness', which includes detailed criteria shown above.

development money spent, to achieve the indicated performance. Technology elasticity answers the question: Will a dollar spent on product development in this arena yield products with significant performance advantages?

2. Business Strength: This strategic dimension is more internally-oriented and focuses on the business's ability to successfully exploit a particular arena. In other words, what does your business bring to the table that suggests that you will be successful in this arena? The ability to leverage your core competencies to your advantage – to attack from a unique position of strength – in the new arena is the key concept here. Business Strength is again a composite dimension or index, consisting of three factors:

1. Ability to leverage technological (development and operations) competencies
2. Ability to leverage marketing and sales competencies

- Gauges 'bang for buck'
- The increase in product performance (or differentiation) versus effort, time or cumulative R&D cost
- Elasticity: % change in product performance to a percentage change in effort (spending)

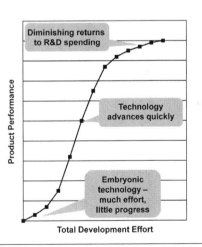

EXHIBIT 4.8: The Technology S-Curve shows how the performance of products based on a technology improves over time (and with more effort). This curve is a useful way of assessing technological opportunities in each arena: those on the steep part offer the most bang for buck.

3. Ability to strategically leverage the potential to achieve product differentiation and competitive advantage.

Exhibit 4.9 shows a more detailed list of criteria that comprise this Business Strength dimension.

Arenas that build on the business's core and distinctive competencies, that fit well the business's marketing and technological strengths and resources, and that offer the business a solid opportunity to gain product and competitive advantage (or achieve product differentiation) are the ones that score high on the Business Strength dimension.

Getting the Information

At this point, management is often tempted to start right away rating various arenas on the two dimensions. In some sessions we've hosted, the executives even wanted to start "voting" on arenas then and there. But the realization quickly set in that they could not, except for areas that were

---

Business Strength

A. Ability to leverage technological competencies, strengths and experience
- Ability to leverage development skills and resources in this arena (technology, IP, R&D or Engineering)
- Degree of fit between operations processes required to succeed in this arena and current operations processes and skills

B. Ability to leverage marketing competencies and strengths
- Ability to leverage existing sales force and/or distribution channel system in this arena
- Ability to leverage existing customer relationships in this arena
- Ability to leverage marketing communications, brand name and promotion assets, approaches and skills in this arena

C. Strategic leverage – potential for gaining product advantage or differentiation
Envision the new products that you would/could develop in this arena; identify some possible entries:
- Would new products here be unique (differentiated from) competitive products?
- Would new products here meet customer needs better than competitive products? A compelling value proposition?
- Would they have a major impact on customers or users in this arena?

EXHIBIT 4.9: Dimension 2 is your 'Business Strength', which includes detailed criteria shown above.

quite close to home. They simply did not have the necessary data to undertake a sound evaluation and rating.

Information has value to the extent that it improves decisions with economic consequences. And what could be more important than the economic consequences of making choices about the right Strategic Arenas? Thus, mini-teams need to be formed to gather the necessary information – to conduct the due diligence needed for management to make intelligent and well-informed decisions on these arenas.

These mini-teams are typically comprised of three people – technical, marketing and operations – and are tasked with getting the information quickly. The detailed criteria, as shown in Exhibits 4.7 and 4.9, provide a guide to the types of information that will be required by senior management. Often, an information template can be constructed from charts like those shown in the exhibits.

After four to eight weeks of data collection, each mini-team prepares a thumbnail sketch of their due-diligence work for one arena, and presents it to senior management. Now senior management is in a much better position to start rating each of the shorted-listed arenas on the two key dimensions shown in Exhibits 4.7 and 4.9.

The Strat-Map: Mapping the Strategic Arenas

How the various arenas score on the two dimensions above can be shown pictorially in the Arena Assessment Map, also known as the Strat-Map, in Exhibit 4.10. "Arena Attractiveness" is shown as the vertical or north-south axis, and "Business Strength" as the horizontal or east-west axis. The result is a four-sector diagram, not unlike traditional business portfolio models, but with quite different dimensions and different components to each dimension.

Each sector represents a different type of opportunity:

- *The best bets* – These are the arenas shown in the north-east sector (upper right). These are the arenas where you should focus your product innovation or R&D efforts. They represent a combination of a positive external environment (attractive markets and solid technological possibilities) and promise strong potential leverage of your core competencies.

- *The conservative bets* – These are in the south-east (lower right) sector. These are the conservative arenas, where your business has strengths but there are limited opportunities for big new products and growth. These opportunities can be pursued at little risk, but offer limited returns. If home-base is here, adopt a "defend the base" strategy for it, and look to other arenas for real growth.

- *The high-risk bets* – These are in the north-west (upper left) sector and are high risk arenas. Very attractive, but you have few exploitable or leveragable strengths here. Consider exploring these arenas with limited spending and, perhaps, via a collaborative entry strategy.

- *No bets* – In the south-west (lower left) sector are the arenas with very poor chances. No spending or entry here!

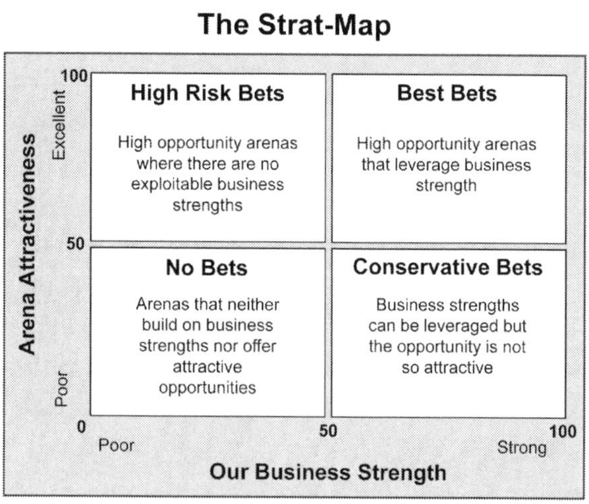

The Strat-Map

EXHIBIT 4.10: Evaluate each arena on the two key dimensions – Arena Attractiveness and your Business Strength. Then locate each arena on a chart like this: your Strat-Map.

Using the Stat-Map, senior management can eliminate certain arenas outright (those in the "no bets" sector) and select a reasonable balance of arenas from the other three sectors. The "best bets" in the north-west sector are usually the top-priority items.

Example: Assessing the arenas at Chempro: At Chempro, Strategic Arena assessment was simplified when management faced the reality of the company's technological and financial resource limitations. Since Chempro's main core competency was its ability to design and engineer rotary hydraulic agitation equipment, embarking on new and expensive technologies (such as bio-oxidation) was deemed out of bounds. Thus, the entire third dimension of Exhibit 4.4 – new technologies – failed on the "feasibility" knock-out question. Moreover, having identified its current technology as a field of particular strength, and recognizing that there are many opportunities to build on this strength, senior management elected to stay with the current technology. Management, thus, chose to attack from a position of strength. So, the third dimension "new technologies" was deleted from the Chempro Strat-Map. The result is the two dimensional matrix in Exhibit 4.5.

Next, data was gathered on 12 arenas plus the home-base. Because Chempro is a medium-sized firm with limited human resources, some of these arenas were researched by the same mini-teams. Management also made available the services of an outside research company to lend a hand digging for the data.

At a strategy session meeting attended by the mini-teams and senior management, the 12 arenas and home-base were rated on the two key dimensions of "Arena Attractiveness" and "Business Strength". A list of rating questions was employed, with each arena rated on each question. The list of rating questions was similar to those shown in Exhibits 4.7 and 4.9. The ratings were added, and both a "Business Strength" and "Arena Attractiveness" index were computed for each of the 13 possible arenas. Using these two indexes for each arena, the 13 arenas were plotted as bubbles on an X-Y grid to yield Chempro's Strat-Map, shown in Exhibit 4.11.

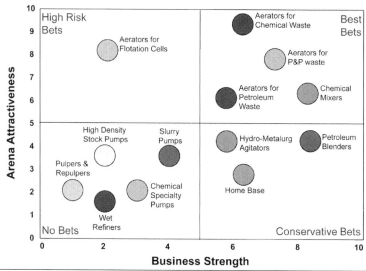

EXHIBIT 4.11: Chempro's Strat-Map shows visually how the various arenas on the 'short list' fare on the two key strategic dimensions.

Picking the Right Arenas

The choice of Strategic Arenas depends on the risk-return values of management. Selecting only those arenas in the top half of the Strat-Map – the best bets and the high-risk bets – emphasizes the attractiveness of the external opportunities. It is a high return, but possibly a higher-risk strategy. This choice places no weight at all on the "Business Strength" dimension: The other extreme is selecting only those arenas to the right of the vertical, the best bets and the conservative bets. It emphasizes selection of only those arenas in which the company possesses a good business position. It is a low-risk, possibly lower-return strategy.

Ideally, you would look for a combination of the two:

- Arenas in which the "Arena Attractiveness" and the "Business Strength" are both rated high – the best bets in the north-east sector of Exhibit 4.10; and,

- A balance of some attractive but riskier arenas with some lower-risk but less attractive ones.

Example: For the Chempro illustration, six arenas fell into the "no bets" sector, including all four pump arenas. These were dismissed immediately. But six other arenas rated positively on both dimensions. In order to quantify or rank order the arenas, a 45-degree diagonal or cut-off line was drawn, as in Exhibit 4.12. Arenas to the right of and above this line were considered positive; those to the left and below were negative. The distance of each arena from that line was measured. The greater the distance, the more desirable the arena.

Based on this exercise, three "best bets" and one "conservative bet" were identified as target arenas for Chempro:

- Aerators for the chemical industry (waste water treatment)
- Blenders for the petroleum industry

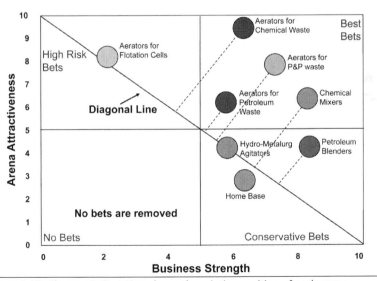

EXHIBIT 4.12: Chempro's Stat-Map shows the relative position of each arena. Those arenas furthest to the top right (with the longest dotted lines) are strategically the best.

- Agitators and mixers for the chemical industry
- Surface aerators for the pulp and paper industry.

In addition, management decided to continue seeking new or improved products in the home-base arena as well, but fairly defensively. With the Strat-Map exercise, the first stage of strategy development was complete. Management was focused on its Strategic Arenas, with a strong sense of their priorities.

Picking the Target Arenas – Wrap-Up

Mapping your battlefields is fundamental to a successful innovation strategy; that is, identify and select the strategic arenas of focus. The previous chapter outlined how to undertake a strategic analysis – first on your industry, marketplace, and your customers' industry; next on yourself – the search for strengths and core competencies that you hope to leverage.

Next, define the potential arenas for your business. Use two dimensions (products and markets, as does Telenor or the pipe manufacturer) or perhaps three dimensions (customer groups, applications, and technologies, like Chempro). Locate your home-base, and then move out on each of the three axes, identifying adjacent customer groups, applications, and technologies. This exercise should help you display a number of new but related possible arenas, as in Exhibit 4.4.

Now that you've identified a list of possible arenas, check each against a set of knock-out questions, and rate each along the two key dimensions: "Arena Attractiveness" and "Business Strength". Develop a list of rating questions for each dimension, and complete the due diligence to obtain the needed data. Then score each arena based on these questions. Draw a Strat-Map (similar to Exhibit 4.10) to see where your arenas lie. Select and prioritize these arenas, looking for those in the desirable "best bets" sector, but perhaps seeking a balance by including one or two from the "sure-bets" and the "high-risk bets" sectors.

Congratulations! You have now decided your Strategic Arenas, the areas on which you will focus your new product development effort. This is a key step. These are the "hunting grounds" for new products; they define what's "in bounds" what's "out of bounds". The battlefields are selected. The next step is deployment. In the following chapter, we will talk about establishing priorities for each arena, making spending decisions on arenas, and crafting attack plans – how to win in each Strategic Arena.

CHAPTER 5

Crafting the Winning Attack Plan

Plans are nothing. Planning is everything.

Dwight D. Eisenhower
Supreme Allied Commander, D-Day, WWII

Developing the Attack Strategies

The goals have been decided, and the Strategic Arenas are mapped out and prioritized. Now it's time to determine the *new product attack strategy* – that is, how you plan to win on these selected battlefields. Attack strategies tend to be fairly industry- and company-specific. However, there exist a number of frameworks that help guide the choice of attack strategies. Here are some of the frameworks or attack plan models we like, but there are certainly others.

Strategy Types Based on Innovativeness

One way of looking at attack strategies is via a typology based upon the way that an organization decides to respond to changing market and external conditions. These strategies are analogous to military strategies, such as an aggressive "frontal attack", versus "out-flanking", versus a more conservative "wait-and-respond" attack strategy.

There are two dimensions to the model, shown in Exhibit 5.1. There are the questions to ask when determining where your business fits on the chart:

1. How important is product innovation to your business? Is innovation front-and-center and a key part of your overall business strategy? Or does your company mostly rely on other strategies for gaining business? For example; does it aim instead for low price, intimate customer relationships, superb service or broad distribution?
2. How proactive versus reactive are you when it comes to innovation? Some firms find the best approach is to let others take the lead, and then to react or defend. Alternatively, others take a more proactive stance.

In Chapter 2, four strategy types were introduced and are based on the model in Exhibit 5.1, each with its own approach to attacking strategic arenas.[1] Which one are you? And which one should you be?[2] Recall the strategy types from Chapter 2:

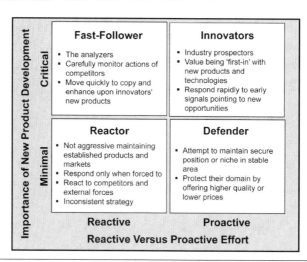

EXHIBIT 5.1: One popular typology of innovation strategy is based on the importance of new products to the business, and whether the firm is proactive or reactive.[1,2]

The Innovators

These businesses are the industry innovators or prospectors. They value being first in with new products and are the first to adopt new technologies, even though there are risks, including that not all efforts will be profitable. Innovators respond rapidly to early signals that point to emerging or new opportunities.

This is a very popular strategy, with about one-third of firms engaged in product development considered to be innovators (Exhibit 5.2).[3] In the automobile business, traditionally Honda and Chrysler are considered to be innovators. For example, in the US auto industry, it was typically Chrysler who created new categories, such as the mini-van and the SUV. Procter & Gamble and Johnson & Johnson are also both considered to be innovators in their respective industries.

Implications of being the innovator: Not every firm can be the industry innovator because innovators must possess certain unique characteristics and strengths. For example, technology, IP or certain technological skills are usually among the core competencies of these businesses. These companies have track records of undertaking leading-edge technological work and, often, there is evidence of fundamental research and true technology development work underway. Typically, these firms are linked to universities and outside labs and by working with these partners, engage in open innovation.

From a marketing standpoint, these innovators strive to stay ahead of the wave, anticipating the next marketing breakthrough. They are excellent at anticipating market needs, and some employ extensive voice-of-customer research, especially ethnography, in order to identify customers' unmet and unspoken needs. They may also work closely with lead users (user-innovators) in the market to seek the next market innovation.

Financially, these innovators are not afraid to make risky investments. Investments tend to be both internal base-business product development as well as external acquisitions and joint ventures.

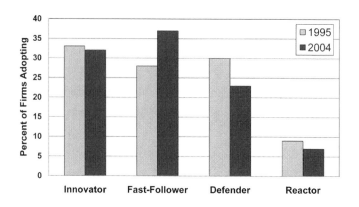

EXHIBIT 5.2: The Fast-Follower strategy is the most popular strategy, just ahead of the Innovator strategy.[3]

Advantages and disadvantages of being an innovator: The advantage of being the innovator is evident. Being first into the market yields competitive advantage, the notion that "first in wins." The problem is that there is no consistent evidence that "first-to-market" wins, unless the second or follower product is a "same as" or parity product. For example, if the innovator sets the industry standard, and all subsequent products must meet that standard (and therefore be identical), then the innovator does fare better. But this is not the situation in most markets. There is considerable evidence that "best in wins"; that the follower company, which develops a superior product, which is not the innovation, tends to do best.

In spite of the lack of consistent evidence about innovators always winning, our research does show an edge for the innovator. Exhibit 5.3 reveals that success rates decline and profitability falls off somewhat with order of market entry. For example, from Exhibit 5.3, note that success rate of development projects drops from about 70 percent for the innovator product (or first into market) to about 63 percent for the second-to-market or fast-follower product. Similarly, profit ratings of new products – profits achieved versus profit objectives – drop somewhat as one moves from the first-in product to later entries.

There are two major challenges to the innovator. The first is risk. Being the pioneer means that no one has gone before to prove the technology or test and develop the market. Often these pioneering development projects are costly, take years to recover the investment, and clearly not every innovative project succeeds. Thus the innovator's executives and shareholders must have an appetite for risk.

The second challenge is that it's not easy: This is leading edge work, both technologically and from a marketing perspective, and not every business finds itself up to the task. Much of the work is an intellectual and physical stretch for technical, production, sales and marketing staff. Johnson & Johnson and Procter & Gamble were cited above as being innovator companies and both are known to hire the "best and the brightest".

Example: Recall the Corning example from the last chapter. Facing a dramatic drop in sales in profits in 2000, Corning's senior management looked to innovation once again – to reinvent itself and its products or face oblivion.[4] Management identified new markets and new technologies and applied its tried-and-proven formula of innovative, pioneering development. And it worked. By 2007, the company was back on its game. Major innovations had been created for each business unit: four new business platforms and three major market adjacencies. The big winner for Corning was glass components of flat screen television screens – a bold and innovative move for Corning, and something its major competitor, Schott Glass in Germany, failed to act on (even though the latter firm was already making CRT tube glass components in 2000).

This Corning case study is an exemplary story of a true innovator facing tough times. Could your company have managed the same feat? It was not easy! Nortel Networks, also heavily into the fiber-optic business (hardware and software), was hit with the same calamitous market

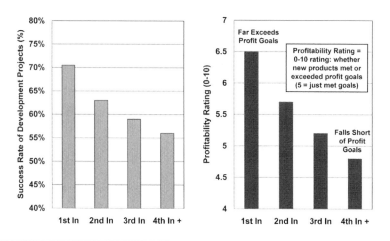

EXHIBIT 5.3: The order-of-entry of new products does have a modest impact on both new product success rates and profitability.

collapse, and saw its share price drop from $140 to less than one dollar; but, where Corning succeeded, Nortel failed to innovate its way out of the abyss, and at this writing is in bankruptcy proceedings.

Fast-followers

These businesses are the analyzers. By carefully monitoring the actions of major competitors, and by moving quickly, they often are able to bring a superior product to market – more cost-efficient or with better features and user-benefits – than the innovator's product. But analyzers are rarely first-to-market.

The fast-follower strategy is the most popular of all strategies, with 37 percent of development firms adopting this approach. The strategy has also gained in popularity, up from 27 percent in a decade, because it is a viable strategy and, at the same time, only moderately risky. In the global automotive business, Toyota and Ford are considered to be fast-followers or analyzer companies although, in the last decade, Toyota has become notably innovative with its hybrid car innovations.

Implications of being the fast-follower: Like innovators, fast-followers must also possess solid technology and a proficient technology group. But the technology and skills are not so much oriented to developing new science and invention — pushing back the frontiers of technology — but rather more to solid engineering, development and applications work. Technology groups in these firms must monitor what is happening technologically in the industry, and identify new technologies that are emerging from the innovators' labs. Once the new technology or new products are identified as prospects for the fast-follower, they must rapidly apply their technological skills to reverse-engineer, copy and improve upon the products.

From a marketing perspective, fast-followers are quite different from innovators. Their job is to monitor the market environment, identifying and qualifying emerging markets and opportunities created by others. Effective competitive analysis and patent mapping are tools these firms use. They closely monitor competitors and their launches, determining which ones hold promise (for example in consumer goods, they employ store audits extensively). Fast-followers use voice-of-customer market research, not to identify entirely new needs or markets, but to uncover potential weakness in and dissatisfactions with innovators' products and to gain insights to improve upon their products. Open innovation is also effectively employed by fast-followers.

Recall the example from Chapter 1, where Apple is the fast-follower in the MP3 market. The company did not invent MP3s, and when Apple entered, there were more than fifty competitors. But by astutely applying its strengths and competencies in technology, marketing and distribution, the company developed a much better product and system that overcame many of the dissatisfactions with the current MP3 products. Apple scored a decisive win.

Financially, fast-followers must be prepared to make substantial investments in R&D and new product projects. But the fast-follower strategy mitigates risk. Because others have gone before, the unknowns and uncertainties – both technologically and in marketing – are not quite as high. Thus, these companies' executives can be somewhat risk averse.

Advantages and disadvantages to being a fast follower: The advantages of the fast-follower strategy are evident. Risk is mitigated, and in some respects the task of developing new products is not quite so daunting for the fast-follower as it is for the innovator. Certainly, a fast-follower must be a proficient product developer, but the pioneer has shown the way, and through the pioneer's successes and mistakes, the fast-follower learns and improves.

The major challenge is that the fast-follower must be exactly that… fast! Too often, followers are "slow followers", taking forever to read the signals of an emerging market or a new technology, and even longer to respond with their own new product. Even then, the response is too often anemic with a product that is not better at all. Thus, the fast-follower must organize to be constantly on top of what is happening in the industry in terms of markets and technology, and then possess an internal "rapid response system" to identify, screen, develop and launch its new product before other competitors have a chance to respond. The worst position is the "middle of the pack".

> *Example:* A major fish processor in Eastern Canada marketed some of its frozen fish product as private label or store-brands in the New England states. (In Canada, the fish company had its own nationally-recognized brand name, but not in the US). Thus a fast-follower strategy proved the preferred approach to the US private-label market. And the modus operandi was clear: "We've got to be the fastest responder you can imagine", declared the company president at the time. "That means, as soon as we spot a national brand product on the shelf in a Boston supermarket on a Friday, by Monday we've got to be working on it; getting the market data, getting samples in our labs, and making a Go/Kill decision".
>
> To facilitate such a rapid-response, the company designed and implemented a fast-response Stage-Gate system that could accelerate projects from idea and concept right through to launch in record time. Extensive store audits coupled with focus groups to dissect competitors' products were two of the tools used in the early stages of this fast-response gating process.

Defenders

Defenders place relatively little emphasis on innovation as a leading edge of their overall business strategy, but they still develop new and improved products. Defenders attempt to locate and maintain a secure position, or niche, in a relatively stable product or market area. They protect their domain by offering higher quality, superior service or lower prices. These businesses ignore industry changes that have no direct influence on their current operations.

Defenders represent about 24 percent of all companies that develop products, but this is declining in popularity as a strategy. One reason is that research reveals a strictly defensive mode is not as successful as a more offensive stance in terms of product innovation performance (Exhibit 5.2). Anecdotal evidence also reveals countless stories of companies that soared because of innovation, and of companies that adopted a strictly defensive position and did not fare well over the long term. They were vulnerable to attack by others; and when markets and technologies changed, they were unwilling or unable to change. General Motors, Nissan and Mazda are defenders. This supports the belief that innovation must be a central facet of your business strategy.

Reactors

These firms are not as aggressive in maintaining established products and markets as competitors. They respond only when forced to by strong external or market pressures. It is difficult to imagine any business deliberately electing this strategy, although some may fall into this quadrant (shown in Exhibit 5.1) by accident. About eight percent of product developers fall into the reactor category.

Which Strategy Type for Your Business?

These four strategy types are useful descriptors when your leadership team is trying to envision the type of product developer your company aspires to be. There are pros and cons to each approach. Thus, you must weigh your own situation: Your marketplace dynamics, your competition, and your own capabilities and competencies before you decide. But be sure to make a conscious choice. Don't just let it happen by default!

Strategy Based on Competitive Dimensions

A second way of visualizing your attack strategy is in terms of fairly traditional competitive dimensions, namely:[5]

- *Competitive scope:* Does your company have an approach that is focused on one or a few market segments? Or, do you serve your market broadly in all segments and all customer types? This is the vertical axis in Exhibit 5.4.
- *Competitive advantage:* How does your firm achieve competitive advantage? Is it achieved thorough low costs, which usually translate

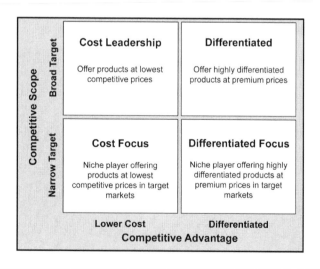

EXHIBIT 5.4: Innovation strategies can also be based on competitive positioning.[5]

into lower prices to the market? Or, do you compete on the basis of product differentiation – developing unique and superior products? This is the horizontal axis in Exhibit 5.4.

Although Exhibit 5.4 shows a standard typology for business strategy types, it also applies to the narrower field of product innovation. Again, four possible strategic types are possible.

Cost Leadership

This strategy emphasizes low manufacturing (or operations) and delivery costs, which are reflected in lower pricing to achieve market share. This strategy can often be combined effectively with the fast-follower strategy; waiting and watching for competitors to launch a new product, then rapidly copying the product, but more cost effectively. Often economies of scale are key to success here: large markets, many segments, with large-volume, low-cost manufacturing facilities. Alternatively, some companies choose operating in lower-cost developing countries as the preferred route to a successful cost leadership strategy.

Cost Focus

A variant of the cost leadership strategy is the focused but low-cost provider. This firm is focused on one market segment, but manages to deliver the product at lower cost. Economies of scale are usually not the method, simply because the single segment does not offer the volume that the cost leadership strategy above demands. However, by uniquely serving a single segment, it may be possible to cut costs and adopt this focused, cost-oriented strategy.

> *Example:* A number of outsourcing companies operating in India have capitalized on that country's well-educated middle class, coupled with their lower wage expectations. These firms have targeted North American and European software firms, and offered their software

development services for a fraction of the cost. By focusing on specific software applications, they have managed to develop and refine their technical skills – an example of a focused cost strategy.

Differentiator

The goal here is to develop unique, superior products – ones that meet customer needs better than competitive products and deliver a compelling value proposition to the user-customer. This approach builds on the very successful strategy identified in one of our strategy studies, Type A Strategy as outlined in Chapter 1, Exhibit 1.8. Strong market orientation (spotting market trends and listening to the voice-of-the-customer) combined with technological prowess are keys to success here.

> *Example:* Black and Decker power tools aimed at the consumer market are the result of this strategy in North America. The business has had a steady stream of differentiated new products from the early days with its *Workmate* bench through to more recent combination power tools, always boasting new features, functionality and design, and always in tune with consumer wants and needs.

Differentiated Focus

The differentiated focus strategy is often called the "niche strategy". The strategy here is to concentrate on one segment or type of user in the marketplace. And you orient your entire product development and marketing effort to uniquely satisfying that target user's needs and desires. Market knowledge and customer intimacy are keys to success here, along with technological capability.

> *Example:* Kenworth trucks, a US manufacturer of heavy-duty highway transport trucks, has traditionally elected this niche strategy. From the beginning, Kenworth has focused on the owner-operator, the independent truck driver who drives his own rig. Everything, from the

traditional and macho truck exterior through to the ability to custom-design and custom-outfit a truck for the discriminating owner, is done to serve this type of buyer.

Other Ways of Visualizing Strategy

The Low Budget Conservative Strategy: In this scenario, a company develops copy-cat, me too, undifferentiated new products, remains highly focused on one or a few product-market areas, and stays close to home. This strategy is described in Chapter 1 as the efficient Type B Strategy in Exhibit 1.9. It is the most popular of all strategy types. By employing this strategy, you ensure that your new products match your business's production, technological skills and resources; and that they fit into your existing product lines and are aimed at familiar and existing markets. R&D spending is usually quite low relative to competitors. This is not a bold strategy, but it produces adequate but not exemplary results.

The Customer-Intimate Strategy: In this case, your business is highly reactive to customer desires, but in a positive way. You respond to specific requests from customers, handling them quickly and effectively. A proficient salesforce, solid relationships with key customers, and a fast-paced, responsive development organization are fundamental to success here.

> *Example:* One major North American consumer paper company (toilet paper, paper towels) operates this way, catering closely to the needs and wishes of its major retailer customers. Most of its product developments are, in fact, responses to requests from these customers. The company has designed an organizational structure and a new product process that enables handling these retailer requests quickly and effectively.

Global versus Local Strategies

One of the most challenging strategic issues for product developers is the global-versus-local dilemma. On the one hand, a global product innovation strategy promises economies of scale. Develop a world product, and then manufacture it in a few large-volume manufacturing facilities. Both development costs and manufacturing costs per unit are minimized. On the other hand, this requires the ability to tailor one's new products to suit differences among regions of the world and differences between countries. Exploiting regional and country difference in tastes, wants and needs is one way to seek a potential for competitive advantage.

Example: In the 1990s, the UK consumer-products firm, Reckitt-Benckiser (then Reckitt & Colman or R&C) faced a global challenge from large US competitors. For years, the firm had competed with unique brands, most of them specific to one or a few countries. They boasted R&D labs in 135 countries. In the US, R&C's brands included cleaning and air freshening products such as Air Wick, Wizard, Easy-Off, Mr. Bubble and later Lysol. In Europe, no one had ever heard of these names, while brands such as Dettol and Harpic reigned. But increasingly, R&C faced competition from US firms such as SC Johnson's Wax and P&G, which began to market US products globally. R&C's advantage had always been the "locally tailored" product, whereas the new US competition had significant cost and brand-leverage advantages.

It was a difficult time for the company, but action was needed. So, R&C elected, and then successfully made, the transition to a "glocal strategy" – developing global products but designed to be customized to suit local tastes, needs and cultures – a "think global, act local" strategy. Thus, an air freshener developed in Hull in the north of England would be rolled out globally, using different brand names, different packaging, and different marketing themes, but essentially the same technology and product platform. The company thereby reaped the advantage of economies of scale in development and manufacturing, but was able to adjust the product to local market requirements around the world.

Finally, there is the argument that, while some domestic suppliers should adopt a more international strategy in product development, such a strategy is not for everyone. There are times when remaining focused on the home market is the winning strategy.

Example: Innovation is viewed in India as "the key to defend their home turf and succeed in global markets",[6] much like the Japanese model; slowly and steadily establishing a unique and large space in global markets by employing product and process innovation. And for the exposed Indian domestic market, the way to stay ahead of imported global products is to leverage local firms' familiarity with, and proximity to, local Indian customers and to create innovative products that better suit local needs.[7]

Global-Local Strategy Dimensions

The two main dimensions of this global-versus-local strategic choice are shown in Exhibit 5.5 and are:

Target Market Strategy: Should your business focus on the home market (domestic), or a regional market (your trade zone, such as North America or Europe), or the global market (the world)?

Product Strategy: Should you adopt a strictly domestic product strategy, developing a product for the home market (which you may later decide to export)?

Or should your business attempt to gain maximum leverage from each new product it develops by adopting a global product strategy? An

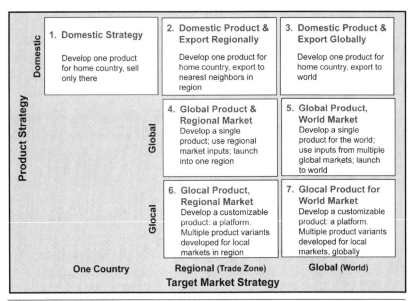

EXHIBIT 5.5: Seven possible international strategies yield very diverse results.

extreme case here would be developing a single product that you market to the entire world, unchanged – "one size fits all".

Or should you instead develop a single but customizable product – a single product platform – from which you then produce different versions of the same product for different regions of the world, or even for specific countries? Your competitive advantage would then be the ability to cater specifically and differentially to the needs and tastes of each region or country, a segmented approach – a "different strokes for different folks" strategy.

Seven Global-Local Strategies

Exhibit 5.5 reveals the seven possible strategies which have been investigated to determine relative efficacy and performance results.[8]

1. Domestic strategy – domestic product sold to domestic target market: This is the least complex of the seven strategies (upper left cell in Exhibit

5.5); it is basically the standard domestic development strategy. You develop products for your home market and sell them only there. The advantage is that the risks and costs are lower, and you can tailor your products to local needs simply because you are local and know the market better than large multinational corporations. Consider the Indian case mentioned above. The disadvantage is that you are vulnerable to international competitors, their economies of scale, and their deep pockets when it comes to R&D spending. Reckitt & Colman's strategy prior to its 1990s transition was essentially this, but in each of 135 countries. This type of strategy leds to performance results that are barely adequate, likely because of the limited market and vulnerability to global competitors: a new product success rate of 43.1 percent and profits falling below objectives, is the average result.

2. Domestic product strategy with export to regional international market: This is an extension of the domestic strategy detailed above. Here a domestic product is developed for your home market without considering international needs and tastes. But then you decide to export the product, perhaps to nearby neighbor countries, expecting a good increase in sales. But this strategy generally leads to barely adequate performance results, likely because of a failure to build in the needs and wants of the nearby, but different, market: a success rate of 45.5 percent and profits failing to meet objectives, on average.

> *Example:* A Swedish seafood company produces pâté-like spreads that go on crackers or bread, and can be used as a breakfast spread. A new fish-based spread was developed for the breakfast market and sold well in Sweden. The developers were quite surprised when they tried to market the same product in nearby Denmark only to see it heartily rejected by the Danes. They had reasoned that Danes are a lot like Swedes, but it seems that Danes were not particularly interested in a strong-tasting fish-spread on their bread at breakfast. They preferred a Danish pastry or a fruit-preserve spread instead.

3. Domestic product strategy with export to global target market: This is the same as Strategy Number 2 above, except attempts are made to give the product even greater international and global reach. It yields equally poor results.

4. and 5. Global product strategy targeted at international market (regional or global): These are "one size fits all" strategies. Here a company develops a new product, either for a region (a trading zone, such as Europe or North America) or for the world, and then markets regionally or globally. The major advantage is economies of scale both in development and manufacturing. And the disadvantage is that you miss differences in local tastes and needs. This strategy, when it can be used, produces positive results: an impressive 61.5 percent success rate with profits meeting objectives on average.

This strategy may also be an elusive one, however, as even products that are thought to be global have some differences country-to-country: McDonalds' Big Mac is not made with beef-hamburger in India, where cattle are sacred animals, they are made from lamb. And even Coke is modified to suit different tastes regarding relative sweetness around the world. Nonetheless certain products, such as standardized commodities (sheet steel, lumber) or technical products (digital cameras for example), are likely global products.

6. and 7. "Glocal" product strategy targeted at international market (regional or global): In these two cases the approach is to develop a single product concept, technology or platform, but seeking multiple international inputs as you do. The resulting product platform can be easily customized so that it is possible to launch multiple variants of a product to suit different regions' or countries' specific needs and tastes. This is the "think global, act local" strategy that R&C elected. The main advantage is that you obtain the best of both worlds: economies of scale on the one hand (a single product concept, platform and technology, perhaps even manufactured in one or a few facilities for the entire world), yet a set of products tailored to suit local market needs. This strategy yields the best results overall: a success rate of 84.9 percent for global markets and 78.1 percent for regional markets, with profits well exceeding objectives.

In practice, electing a glocal strategy means defining the market as an international or global one, and designing products to meet multiple international requirements. This usually means utilizing a transnational product development team for the development project, with team members seconded from around the world. It also requires conducting and seeking customer inputs and insights from multiple international markets. The result is a "glocal" product: one development effort by one team, one product concept or platform, but several product variants to satisfy different international markets.

A major implication of this strategy is the need to design and implement a transnational new product process and system that all your business units around the world utilize, and that integrates actions across country borders. A transnational development process has a number of challenges:

- Ideas for new products must be solicited from many countries, not just from the home country
- Ideas need to be screened and prioritized via a global project prioritization (or portfolio management) group and process
- Global gatekeeping or Go/Kill decision-making groups need to be established – where senior managements from multiple countries make the decision to move ahead together, and jointly fund the project
- Global criteria for Go/Kill and project prioritization decisions replace the traditional single-country criteria.

The major challenge here is integrating the inputs – needs, wants, preferences – from multiple countries into a single, albeit customizable, product concept or platform. At times there are conflicts. For example, part of the world wants a low-cost product; the rest of the world wants a premium product. So there is a conflict that might result in a seriously compromised product design that serves neither group well. Thus, a facet of this "glocal" strategy might be a decision to have two customizable platforms for the same product category. The key here is to operate with facts – get the market knowledge and insights up front – and then you are in a much better position to make the trade-offs needed and define the product concept(s) and the required platforms.

Performance Results Speak for Themselves

New product success rates are profoundly affected by the particular international strategy selected. For example, as noted above, the "glocal" strategy – new products with international input and design, custom-tailored, but aimed at world markets – achieves an enviable 84.9 percent success rate. Unfortunately, only 17 percent of new product projects follow this strategy.

Conversely and not surprising, the most popular strategy is the domestic product strategy. About one third of all new products are classified into this strategy-type – products aimed at only the domestic market. Here, the success rate falls to a low of 43 percent.

The message is this: On all performance measures, products that are designed to meet international requirements (versus only domestic) and that are targeted at international markets – either worldwide or regional – are the top performers, and by a considerable margin. As expected, these products do better in foreign markets, but they also do better at home! And most importantly, they do better overall in terms of profitability and meeting sales and profit targets. These results make a strong case for adopting an international orientation – either global or "glocal" – in product design and development efforts.

Multiple Strategies Under the Same Roof?

A question we are frequently asked is: Can a business have multiple innovation strategies at the same time? For example, can a business be an innovator on some products and a fast-follower on others? Generally the answer is: "yes, but…" That is, some of the strategies outlined above can indeed be combined, and there may even be advantages to doing so. Thus a strategy from Exhibit 5.1 – for example, the "fast-follower" – can be combined with a strategy from Exhibit 5.4 – "cost leadership" – and with a strategy from Exhibit 5.5 – Number 4, "global product, regional market". Generally, strategies chosen from the different exhibits (5.1, 5.4 and 5.5) are not mutually exclusive.

Strategies from the same Exhibit, however, do tend to be mutually exclusive. For example, a company can adopt a "differentiated" strategy for a new product, or a "cost-focused" strategy, but not both together for that product. Moreover, these mutually exclusive strategies should not be employed under the same roof, even on different products or product categories. The reason: Cultures, organizational design and systems required for the different strategies are so specific to each that conflicts are almost guaranteed. For example, the low-cost provider culture is very different than the differentiator culture in Exhibit 5.4. Likely, the two would have trouble existing in the same business. The exception is this: If the two groups can be physically separated and provided the opportunity to develop their own cultures, systems, methods and organizational designs, then it will likely work.

> *Example:* The fish processor cited earlier has three quite different businesses or markets. One is the stores brand or private label New England business, for which the CEO elected a "fast-follower strategy". But his Canadian national brand, a leading and well-known brand sold in supermarkets in that country, requires a "differentiated, premium" and "innovator" strategy. Finally, the third business is food service – hotels and restaurants. For this segment, he adopts a "low-cost" and "customer intimate" strategy.
>
> The only way these three very different strategies can co-exist in the same corporation is to literally put them under different roofs: To set up three separate business units, each with its own physical premises, each with its own systems (different versions of Stage-Gate for example, and different market insight methods), and each with its own culture.

Note that the strategies within each business in this example are not in conflict: For example, for the Canadian national branded products, the strategies "differentiated premium" from Exhibit 5.4 and "innovator" from Exhibit 5.1 are synergistic and work together.

Chempro's Attack Strategy

The Chempro case was used to illustrate the correct selection of strategic arenas in the previous chapter. But what should Chempro's attack plans be? What strategy should the firm select to win in these arenas?

Example continues: Chempro's management elects a general attack strategy that is the same across all arenas. It is a differentiated approach which focuses on delivering superior products with unique product features and improved performance for customers. This strategy requires a marriage of Chempro's core technology competency (prowess in the field of rotary hydraulic equipment design) coupled with a customer-orientated, market-driven approach to defining product requirements. Thus, the strategy is really a combination of the "fast-follower" strategy in Exhibit 5.1 and the "differentiated" strategy in Exhibit 5.4.

Deciding Your Entry Strategies

The previous chapter focused on selecting the right arenas and gaining the right focus. And the current chapter, so far, has dealt with the question: How should you attack each new product arena – what's your attack strategy? Another equally important question is: By what mechanism should you enter these arenas to avoid failure and to maximize gain? Although these questions are fundamentally different, note that they should not be answered independently of one another.[9] Entering a new Business Arena may be achieved by a variety of mechanisms, such as

Licensing – in and out	A formal legal agreement where one firm sells IP, technology or a product for use or sale by another firm, usually for a fixed fee and royalty.
Joint venture	A formal legal arrangement between partners in a joint development and/or business initiative. Risks and rewards are negotiated and shared formally.
Co-development	Working with outside partners in the development of new products and/or services. Can be a subset of joint venturing or open innovation initiative. May include peer-to-peer or supplier/customer co-development.
Open innovation	Collaborative development which includes the broad concepts of leveraging all external sources of ideas, technology and innovation to drive internal growth. Also entails the spin-off and outsourcing of unused intellectual property.
Collaborative innovation	Similar to open innovation and co-development, but can also include formal networks or consortia that come together in an alliance to study common issues and/or develop new products and services.
Open source	Derived from the term used in the software development industry, where informally structured collaborations take place (usually without ownership or remuneration) to create a shared outcome from which all can benefit. Similar to crowd-sourcing, but not owned by any one corporation.
Educational acquisition	Where a large firm purchases a small high technology firm in order to learn more about a technology, acquire the technology, and/or to gain a first entry at low cost.
Venture capital and venture nurturing	Where the firm invests capital in a smaller, usually high technology firm and takes an ownership position. In the nurturing model, management in the large firm plays an active role in managing the smaller firm, playing mentoring or nurturing role.

EXHIBIT 5.6: The are many models for engaging external partners in product innovation. Use this list for your options.

internal development, joint ventures, various forms of open innovation, and minority investments of venture capital. Exhibit 5.6 provides a thumbnail summary of the many options you have. And each of these mechanisms makes unique demands upon your business.[10]

Exhibit 5.7 shows an entry strategy selection framework based on the popular model of market and technological newness and familiarity. It provides a guide to selecting the right entry strategies:[11]

1. *Technology Newness:* How new is the technology to your company – the degree to which the technology is different from that found in the products your company currently produces.

2. *Market Newness:* How new is the market to your company – the degree to which your company's products are not sold into that particular market.

3. *Technology Familiarity:* The degree to which knowledge of the technology exists within your company, but is not necessarily found in its current products.

4. *Market Familiarity:* The degree to which a market is known by your company, but not necessarily as a result of selling into that market.

If the business in which the firm currently competes is defined as its base business, then the markets associated with the new arena may be characterized as base, new familiar or new unfamiliar (see the vertical axis in Exhibit 5.7). The same is true for technology: The degree to which technology is required in your arena is either base, new but familiar to you or new and unfamiliar (see the horizontal axis in Exhibit 5.7).

The thesis underlying this framework is that the newer or less related an arena is to the base business, the poorer the results to the firm if it tries to undertake the venture without help. This leads to the logical conclusion that entry strategies requiring high corporate involvement should be reserved for new arenas with familiar markets and familiar technologies. Similarly, entry mechanisms requiring low corporate input (seeking outside help or collaborative efforts) seem best for unfamiliar arenas. For

Technologies Embodied in the Products

	Base	New, familiar	New, unfamiliar
New, unfamiliar	Joint Ventures	Venture Capital or Venture Nurturing or Educational Acquisitions	Venture Capital or Venture Nurturing or Educational Acquisitions
New, familiar	Internal Market Development or Acquisitions (or Joint Ventures)	Internal Ventures or Acquisitions or Licensing	Venture Capital or Venture Nurturing or Educational Acquisitions
Base	Internal Product Development (or Acquisitions)	Internal Product Development or Acquisitions or Licensing	Joint Ventures (often large firm with small firm)

Market Targeted by the Products

EXHIBIT 5.7: Optimum entry strategies are recommended for different types of arenas, depending on their market and technological "newness" to the firm.[9]

example, the automotive pipe manufacturer in Chapter 3 entered a new and unfamiliar market (household plumbing fixtures) with its base technology (quick-connect fittings), and did so successfully by way of a joint venture relationship with a major plumping fixture manufacturer.

Various entry strategies are shown in the matrix in Exhibit 5.7 for different degrees of market and technological newness. The matrix is supported by case histories, showing the success-failure patterns across the matrix. Note, for example, the cell in Exhibit 5.7 for new markets but base technologies (upper left) points to a joint venture entry strategy – the pipe manufacturer apparently made the right choice. The various entry strategies shown in Exhibit 5.7 are explained in more detail below. The advantages and disadvantages of each are summarized in Exhibits 5.8 and 5.9.

Internal Development: Internal development exploits internal resources as a basis for establishing a new business or entering a new arena. This is a "do it yourself" approach to product development. But a lack of familiarity with markets and technologies in the new business arena often leads to major errors and is one reason for poor performance.[12] Internal developments are recommended only for base business arenas; for those involving new but familiar markets using base technologies; or, those using new but familiar technologies targeted at base markets (the three lower left cells in Exhibit 5.7).

Acquisitions: Acquisitions may be attractive, not only because of speed of execution, but because they might offer a much lower cost of entry into a new arena. Acquisitions are appropriate for new but familiar arenas, as shown in Exhibits 5.7 and 5.8. But words of warning: Not all acquisitions end up as profitable as initially projected. Many prove difficult and costly to integrate into the culture and operations of the acquiring company.

Licensing: Acquiring technology through licensing represents an alternative to acquiring a complete company. Licensing avoids the risk of product development by exploiting the experience of firms that have already developed and marketed the product.[13] Licensing is particularly appropriate when entering new but familiar technology arenas.

Entry Strategy	Advantages	Disadvantages
Internal Development	• Uses existing resources • Familiar markets and technology – fewer surprises, more experience	• Resources may be tied up on other projects • Time lag to break-even may be long • Unfamiliarity with some markets may lead to business errors
Acquisition	• Rapid market entry	• New business area unfamiliar to parent • Acquisitions are often costly • Merging two cultures can be problematic, time-consuming and costly
Licensing	• Rapid access to proven technology and product designs • Reduces financial exposure	• Not a substitute for internal competence • Not propriety technology – you are dependent on licensor

EXHIBIT 5.8: These three entry strategies have both advantages and disadvantages. Refer to Exhibit 5.7 to see when each is best applied.

Internal Ventures: Many companies adopt new venture strategies in order to meet ambitious plans for diversification and growth.[14] In this strategy, a firm attempts to enter different markets or attempts to develop substantially different products from its base businesses by setting up a separate entity within the existing corporate body. The concept is to establish small businesses – entrepreneurial, venture businesses – within the large corporation, taking advantage of the corporation's resources, but freeing the venture team from the usual corporate barriers to entrepreneurial behavior.

Joint Ventures or Alliances: When projects get larger, technology too expensive, and the cost of failure too large to be borne alone, joint venturing becomes increasingly viable.[15] Often the joint venture occurs where a large and a small company join forces to create a new entry in the marketplace (upper left cell in Exhibit 5.7). In these efforts of "mutual pursuit", usually without the formality of a joint venture company, the small firm provides the technology, the large enterprise provides the marketing capability, and the venture is synergistic for both parties. Large-company, small-company alliances, called "strategic partnering", often involve the creative use of corporate venture capital.[16]

Venture Capital and Nurturing: The venture strategy that permits some degree of entry, but the lowest level of corporate commitment, is that associated with external venture capital investment. Major corporations invest venture capital in developing or start-up firms in order to become involved in the growth and development of such firms, and may eventually acquire them outright. The motivation is to secure a "window on technology" by making minority investments in young, growing, high-technology enterprises. When the investing company provides managerial assistance as well as venture capital to the small firm, the strategy is classed as "venture nurturing" rather than pure venture capital. This nurturing strategy appears a more sensible entry in achieving diversification objectives as opposed to simple provision of funds, but it also needs to be tied to other company diversification efforts.[17]

Educational Acquisitions: Targeted small acquisitions can fulfill a role similar to that of a venture capital minority investment and, in some circumstances, offer significant advantages. In such an acquisition, the large firm acquires a small firm, usually with an "interesting technology" at the early stage of development. The acquisition is made, not so much for financial return reasons, but to acquire know-how and familiarity at minimal cost. Here the acquiring firm immediately obtains people familiar with the new technology area whereas, in a minority investment, the parent company relies on its existing staff to build familiarity by interacting with the investee. Acquisitions made for educational purposes may therefore represent a faster route to familiarity than the venture capital "window" approach and are recommended as one possible entry strategy for new, unfamiliar arenas (top right cell in Exhibit 5.7).

Towards "Open Innovation": All the collaborative and partnering entry strategies outlined above – joint ventures, licensing, alliances, venture nurturing – are a subset of a broader innovation strategy, namely "open innovation" which is highlighted in the next section. Innovation via partnering with external firms and people has been around for decades. "Open innovation" is simply a broader concept that includes not only these traditional partnering models but *all types of collaborative or partnering* activities, and with a wider range of partners than in the past.

Entry Strategy	Advantages	Disadvantages
Internal Venture	• Uses existing resources • Enables company to retain and foster talented entrepreneurs	• Mixed success record • Company's internal climate often unsuitable and non-supportive
Joint Venture or Alliance	• Technology/marketing unions can exploit large-company/small-company synergies • Distributes risk	• Potential for conflict between partners; cultural differences • Sometimes surprises about each other's capabilities and commitment
Venture Capital and Nurturing	• Can provide window in new technology or market	• Unlikely to be a major stimulus for company growth
Educational Acquisitions	• Provides window, knowledge and initial staff	• Higher initial financial commitment than venture capital • Risks the departure of (acquired) entrepreneurs

EXHIBIT 5.9: These additional four entry strategies have advantages and disadvantages. (Exhibit 5.7 shows when to use each strategy.)

Open Innovation's Role in Your Strategy

Firms such as P&G have seized on the concept of open innovation and have made it an integral part of their product innovation strategy. "While there is no best way to structure an innovation centered company, it is clear that the sun is setting on the internally focused, vertically integrated organization", declares A.G. Lafley, Chairman and CEO of Procter & Gamble. "We are in the era of the open corporation".[18]

As a result, P&G's "Connect + Develop" open innovation approach is now a major part of that company's innovation strategy, structure, culture and processes. And it brings in more than 50 percent of the company's new product ideas and technology – and in some cases – fully developed new products ready for commercialization. Open innovation is one strategic approach that you should consider as a means to entering or attacking new arenas (and also for expanding horizons in existing Strategic Arenas). Thus, this chapter would not be complete without exploring how open innovation may benefit your business.

The Threat

Major corporations face a major threat – the fact that their own internal R&D has not been the engine of innovation in their industries, and that they have missed opportunity after opportunity. Indeed, many of the breakthrough products over the last decades have come from outside major corporations.[19] IBM sat by and watched as others innovated with minicomputers, workstations, PCs and palm computers; P&G failed to launch a major new consumer brand for almost 20 years; Merck watched Pfizer seize the lead in the drug industry by marketing compounds that were usually licensed from other companies' laboratories; American Express watched others create the cash management account, the debit card, and internet payment systems; and AT&T witnessed microwave relay transmission, global positioning systems, satellite transmission, and packet switching technologies emerge far from its Bell Labs.[20] Some of the reasons why dominant firms seem to lack peripheral vision or fail to act on disruptive technologies were outlined in Chapter 4. Open innovation is one solution to this failure to see and act in time.

"Not all of the smart people in your industry work for you," is the premise for open innovation.[21] Too much invention and innovation takes place outside of your walls to ignore; and many ideas, inventions and innovations come from smaller, entrepreneurial start-ups funded by venture capitalists.[22] Many of these create breakthrough technologies, ideas and new business models to disrupt established categories and markets. Thus, today's competitive advantage often comes from leveraging the discoveries of others. The implication of that trend is unavoidable: "You cannot meet your growth objectives if you ignore all of the smart people out there who are not on your payroll".[23]

Does your organization suffer too much from NIH – the "not invented here" syndrome? Leading companies have recognized the need for open innovation – for a healthy balance between internally and externally generated ideas and new products. And they have put in place the processes, IT support, teams and culture to leverage external partners and alliances in their quest for new ideas, inventions and innovations. The goals of open innovation are to create new products in untapped "white spaces", to gain access to new technologies, to speed development projects to market, and to create more value from internally generated technologies by selling off or licensing out unused internal intellectual property.

Open Versus Closed Innovation

In the traditional or closed innovation model, inputs come from both internal and external sources: Customer inputs, marketing ideas, marketplace information or strategic planning inputs. Then the process shifts inward, as the firm's R&D organization invents, evolves and perfects technologies for further development, either immediately or at a later date.[24]

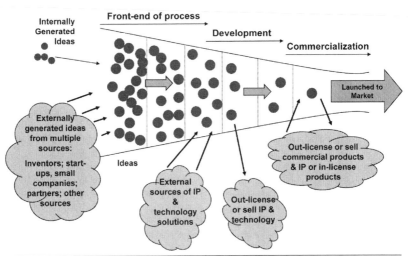

EXHIBIT 5.10: Companies heavily engaged in Open Innovation have re-designed their traditional gating or Stage-Gate processes to build in the necessary actions and elements for seeking ideas, technology, IP and even ready-to-commercialize products from outside the company.

Example: It was these technologies "on-the-shelf" that led to so much criticism of Xerox for its failure to commercialize many of its inventions in the computer field. While the shareholders of Xerox did not benefit, others did. Employees who worked on promising technologies left to form start-up companies, many of which (such as 3Com and Adobe) achieved huge success. In fact, the market capitalization of Xerox's spin-offs exceeded that of Xerox itself.[25]

By contrast, in open innovation, companies look inside-out and outside-in, across all three aspects of the innovation process, including ideation, development, and commercialization (Exhibit 5.10). In doing so, much more value is created and realized throughout the process.

Many Models for Open Innovation

Open innovation has been implemented in a variety of ways in different companies. Here are some examples:

Procter & Gamble: Open innovation has had one of its most successful implementations at Procter & Gamble. The entire world has now become P&G's source of innovation ideas, IP and ready-to-commercialize new products through its highly successful "Connect + Develop" initiative.[26] Using IT, a well-crafted and user-friendly webpage, coupled with an organizational structure and culture that supports external collaboration, IP and ideation, P&G has opened its doors to would-be innovators, idea-people, inventors, scientists, collaborators and problem-solvers from around the world.

Air Products and Chemicals: The company's "Identify and Accelerate" initiative identifies internal needs and then the role that external partnering can play to accelerate the innovation process.[27] Most of the emphasis is on securing outside R&D resources to work on the company's own development projects.

Nokia Venturing: Nokia has moved beyond "not invented here" and is embracing the best ideas wherever they are, using a multi-faceted approach:[28]

- Nokia's Venturing Organization undertakes venturing activities designed to identify and develop new businesses for the renewal of the corporation
- Nokia Venture Partners invests exclusively in mobile and IP related startup businesses
- Nokia's Innovent Group directly supports and nurtures nascent innovators with the hope of growing future opportunities.

Spalding: In this commodity sporting goods category, Spalding is reinvigorating the company through innovation, including technology developed externally. Spalding introduced the "Infusion", the first basketball with a built-in pump, which led to a 32 percent increase in sales[29] and the "Never-Flat" basketball, technology developed by Primo Innovations, a small invention company founded by two PhDs from NASA and DuPont.

Technology Out-licensing: Caterpillar, Sharp, Kimberly Clark, Philips, and P&G are all examples of companies that out-license internally developed intellectual property. The benefits include value derived from otherwise unused knowledge, and the development of useful strategic partnerships.

The Benefits of Open Innovation

Open innovation suddenly makes viable those Strategic Arenas you may have considered but walked away from because you lack what it takes to succeed. Open innovation allows your business much greater access to the talent, skills, technology, and know-how needed for product development, particularly in some of the new-new arenas in Exhibit 5.7 – far beyond what your own internal technical or market groups can provide. Thus, the prospect of open innovation not only changes your entry strategies, but impacts on your choice of arenas in the first place. For example, the GPS company in Chapter 4 rejected the arena "radio signal transmission tower for mobile phones" because it was just too big for them to handle. This was the correct decision. But because they are an open and collaborative company, they were indeed able to define two other arenas: "control systems for the entire constellation of satellites" and "space born receivers" (on a satellite to improve accuracy and positioning). They could target these arenas provided they worked openly with a consortium of partner companies.

Another obvious benefit of open innovation is the much larger base of ideas and technology from which to draw to drive internal growth in your existing Strategic Arenas.[30] Additionally, the risk in developing truly innovative products is reduced through a shared risk model. The firm can conduct strategic experiments at lower levels of risk and resources, with the opportunity to extend core business and create new sources of growth. Over time, a more innovative culture is created – from the outside in – through continued exposure and relationships with external innovators. Finally, by licensing-out or selling unused products, technology and IP, companies not only capture economic value from their ideas, but they create a sense of urgency internally to "use it or lose it" when it comes to their own internally available technologies.

Collaborative approaches, joint ventures and strategic alliances are on a growth path because companies' prosperity and growth depend upon them. The great majority – 64 percent of surveyed US executives – indicate that they plan to increase their use of strategic alliances during the next two years;[31] and almost 70 percent of the executives said that strategic alliances help companies reach growth objectives, in part, because they promised attractive returns and shared risk.

Not a Bed of Roses

The major challenge with open innovation and an open webpage invitation to the world is the costs of implementing the system. P&G employs a small army of people to read, review, evaluate and follow up on the thousands of new product and idea submissions they receive. One of its major European competitors finally gave up on open innovation, finding that the results obtained were not worth the cost and effort. There are other negatives too: Open innovation may suit consumer goods firms, such as Spalding, P&G and Kimberly Clark, where products are relatively simple, but in more complex product industries, open innovation maybe less useful. As GE's Chief Executive observes, his firm is a leader in fields like jet engines and locomotives, which requires "doing things that almost nobody else in the world can do", and where intellectual property rights and a degree of secrecy still matter.[32] Mark Little, Head of GE Research, is even more skeptical and professes great satisfaction with the output of GE's own research laboratories, "We're pretty happy with the hand we've got". Toyota's senior executive adds that, with the billions of dollars his firm spends on research – not to mention a five year product development cycle – it would be foolish to open up and allow rivals to steal its edge. "Eventually even Google will have to make something tangible, and when they do, they will protect it – just like Toyota, which does not have an open model."

So while open innovation may seem like an inexpensive method of new product generation, the cost is far from free; indeed, it is very resource intensive. And there are other negatives. As noted by professors at London's Imperial College, "The costs of open innovation, in management distraction or lost intellectual property rights, are not nearly as well studied as its putative benefits".[33] The fact is that one must wade through a lot of mediocre ideas and product submissions to find a few gems, and it's the wading through that takes the work.

Winning Attack Plans: Wrap-Up

You have selected one or more Strategic Arenas as a target. Now: How are you going to win in that arena? Here is how to develop an outline of your attack strategies:

- What is your strategic stance: innovator, fast-follower, defender, or reactor?
- What competitive strategy do you choose: low-cost provider, differentiator, or focused niche player?

- Or perhaps, you have chosen a strategy that is not on the two-dimensional charts: the customer-intimate strategy or the low budget conservative strategy.
- Decide your strategic approach to deal with the global-versus-local issue: A regional or global target market approach? A global or "glocal" product innovation strategy?
- Next, address how you plan to enter the strategic arena you have chosen: Will it be alone, via acquisition, licensing, with alliance partners, or in a joint venture?
- Decide what role you wish open innovation to play in your innovation strategy.

With arenas defined and with attack strategies in place, it's time to turn to the challenging issue of resources. Translating your strategy into reality means deployment of resources: How many resources, and where to allocate them. This is the topic of the next chapter.

Resource Commitment, Deployment and Strategic Buckets

> You gotta know when to hold 'em
> Know when to fold 'em
> Know when to walk away
> Know when to run
>
> Kenny Rogers, *The Gambler*

Optimizing Your New Product Investments

Much like stock market portfolio managers, those senior executives who optimize their R&D investments – by committing the right resources, focusing these resources on the right Strategic Arenas, selecting winning new product projects, and achieving the ideal balance and mix of projects – will win in the long run. There are two facets to new product resource optimization.

1. Determining the right level of investment in product innovation: Has your business committed sufficient resources to achieve your new product goals and objectives? Or, are you heavily under-resourced in product innovation and face tough decisions regarding resource commitments for the future? Many executives struggle with the issue: How much is enough? And with today's business pressures to cut expenditures of all types, R&D spending comes under scrutiny. So the question of determining the optimal investment level for new products or R&D is the topic for the first part of this chapter.

2. Managing the portfolio of new products: A vital and related question is this: Are you strategically allocating your scarce and valuable new product resources correctly – to the right markets, product types and major projects? That is what portfolio management is all about: resource allocation and investment decisions to achieve your business's new product objectives.[1] Strategic Portfolio Management is a major topic of this and the next chapter.

Resource Commitment – A Decisive Factor in the Innovation War

You cannot win a war without resources in the field! Or as one executive succinctly put it: "You gotta spend money to make money!" Committing sufficient resources to product innovation, and then allocating the resources effectively, is one of the four points of performance on the Innovation Diamond introduced in Chapter 1 (Exhibit 1.1). And how astutely and strategically you and your leadership team commit and allocate these resources is one of the main differences between the best and worst performing businesses.[2]

A resource crunch exists in product innovation today.[3] Our benchmarking study found that major resource deficiencies in new product development are widespread. Management has failed strategically in the great majority of corporations and has not committed sufficient resources to achieve the lofty objectives it has set for product innovation, nor to execute the projects in the development pipeline in a proficient and timely fashion.[4] Too many companies fail to recognize that spending on product innovation is a strategic investment, not an expense. Hence they create this resource crunch in product innovation by allocating insufficient resources to undertake the projects they should.

A lack of project focus and inadequate resources surfaces in our study as the number one weakness in product development efforts: Project teams are working on too many projects, or are not sufficiently focused on new product work (Exhibit 6.1). Consider these findings:

- Only 10 percent of businesses properly staff new product projects – resources are simply inadequate in 90 percent of firms to enable project teams to do a quality job!
- In only 11 percent of businesses are teams focused on their projects; 89 percent confess that project team members are spread too thinly over too many projects. (Multi-tasking is fine up to a point, but clearly the point of multi-tasking for optimum efficiency has been far exceeded in many businesses.)
- Almost 80 percent of businesses note that team members are doing far too many "other tasks" as well as struggling to work on new product projects.
- A minority of businesses – 38 percent – are attempting to rectify the resource crunch by setting up dedicated or "ring-fenced" innovation teams to staff major new product projects.

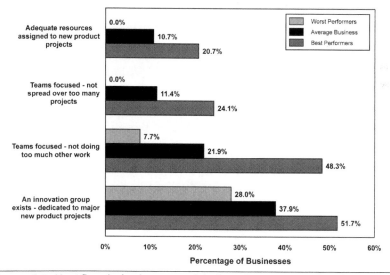

EXHIBIT 6.1: Most firms lack adequate and dedicated resources assigned to development projects. Top performers devote more.[2]

A close examination of the many reasons for new product failure, coupled with results from recent benchmarking studies, shows that many of these failure modes are traceable to a much more fundamental cause, namely major resource deficiencies.[5] For example, poor quality of execution and leaving out important tasks (like voice-of-customer) is often not due to ignorance or a lack of willingness. It is more often because of a lack of people and time. As one senior project leader declared, "We don't deliberately set out to do a bad job on projects. But with my seven major projects underway, I'm being set up for failure... there just isn't enough time to do a solid job... and so I cut corners."

A lack of resources devoted to product innovation is not just an R&D or one-function problem; it is pervasive, cutting across all functional boundaries (Exhibit 6.2).[6] The weakest areas are marketing resources (only 15.2 percent of businesses have sufficient marketing resources devoted to new product projects), followed by manufacturing and operations resources for new products (only 24.3 percent have sufficient resources for new products). R&D or technical resources is the best resourced area, with 31.4 percent of businesses indicating sufficient technical resources are in place – still weak, but better than the other functions.

Top Performers Dedicate Resources to Product Innovation

Top performing businesses are much more resource rich in product innovation than other businesses – they commit the resources to product innovation necessary to get the job done, as shown in Exhibit 6.1. And more: Top performers' project teams are much more focused and dedicated to product development. Indeed, having the necessary resources in place, and ensuring that these resources are properly dedicated and focused, is one of the strongest discriminators between the best performing businesses and the rest.[7]

Resource commitment is also more cross-functional in top performing business, much more so than in other businesses. It is not just a matter of having R&D players on the field. Exhibit 6.2 reveals that top performers

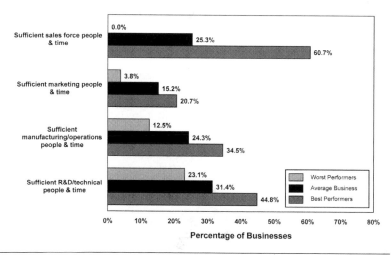

EXHIBIT 6.2: The percentage of businesses that devote adequate resources to product innovation is broken down by department. Marketing resources are the weakest.[2]

are much more likely to commit sufficient resources from marketing, sales, operations, as well as R&D. Note that the greatest difference between best and worst businesses is for sales resources: In top performing companies, salespeople are made available to work on new product project teams. In the poor performers this is not the case.

This data on the impact of resource commitments confirms an earlier study, where resource deficiencies in all areas – R&D, marketing, sales and operations – were identified as significantly and seriously deficient when it came to product innovation.[8] Further, adequate resources devoted to new product development is one of the three strongest drivers of new product performance. The *strongest single driver* of the most commonly used performance metric - percentage of sales from new products – is how much the business spends on R&D!

Insufficient Resources Cripple Product Innovation Efforts

A lack of new product resources leads to many fatal ailments in product innovation efforts.[9] How many does your business suffer from?

1. Poor Quality of Execution: When resources on projects are tight, corners are cut as project teams scramble to meet timelines. Thus, essential market studies are truncated, up-front homework is short-circuited, field trials are overly accelerated, and launch plans are thrown together and under resourced. As one frustrated executive put it: "We're so busy just getting the projects done – marching to a timeline – that we don't have the time for any of this important up-front work".

Research into new product practices reveals poor quality of execution on project tasks from idea right through to launch.[10] Poor quality of execution ultimately results in lower new product success rates and too much "fix and repair" work (activities done in haste come back to haunt the project team, necessitating much rework).[11]

2. Lengthened Time-to-Market: With not enough resources to handle the many projects in the pipeline, queues begin to build. The idea-to-launch time is not so much execution time, as it is queuing time or WIP (work in process), waiting for people to find the time to do the work. One estimate is that queuing time is 30 to 50 percent of project cycle time.[12] Get rid of the queues and you could cut time-to-market by as much as half!

3. Too Few Game-Changers: New product failures and being late to market are the measurable costs of poor or untimely execution, often brought on by insufficient resources. A far greater cost is not measurable, because it is an opportunity cost. How many projects are simply not done due to a lack of resources? Given limited resources, human nature dictates that they be used on lower risk initiatives that don't cost very much. As one executive explained, "My business has a limited R&D budget. I can't afford to risk a major percentage of that budget on a handful of big projects. I've got to hedge my bets and pick the smaller and lower risk ones. If I had a larger R&D budget, then I might tackle some more venturesome projects."

Lacking the resources to do an effective job, technical and marketing executives start to favor smaller, easier-to-do and faster projects – the "low-hanging fruit". The trouble is they are often low value to the company. The immediate result is a lack of blockbuster or game-changer projects in the pipeline. Indeed, 45 percent of executives confess having too many low value projects in their development portfolios, and 69 percent indicate a poorly balanced portfolio of projects.[13,14]

4. Active Projects are "Dumbed Down": Another result of resource deficiencies is that projects are "dumbed down" or de-scoped. One R&D leader described the resource deficiency this way, "Heroic efforts can only compensate for the resource gap for so long. So they [the project teams] make the projects simpler: They de-scope the project, and de-feature the product... they simply don't build in all the product features and functionality that they know they should." And so de-scoping and de-featuring takes its toll on potentially great new products.

5. Poor Project Team Morale: Inadequate resources also impact the project team. Faster time-to-market and cycle time reduction are paramount themes in many businesses. But, lacking the necessary personnel and their time commitments from functional bosses, the project team is stretched. Deadlines are missed, pressure mounts, people are blamed, and team morale starts to deteriorate:[15]

Example: In one business investigated, so bad was the morale of project teams that no one wanted to be on future teams. Being put on a product development team was viewed as a punishment. The reason: There was so much time pressure on these teams to accomplish the impossible, and so few resources to do the work, that teams were destined to fail. And they were being chastised by management.

How Much Is Enough – Deciding the Investment Level for Your Product Innovation Effort

Four fundamental approaches are available to help you, the leadership team of the business, decide how many resources to commit to product development or how much to invest in R&D.

The methods detailed below are not mutually exclusive and can be used in conjunction with each other. Let us look at each approach:

1. Investment Level Based on the Strategic Role of Your Business

This top-down method is premised on the simple tenet that your business strategy should drive your product innovation or R&D spending. It is a particularly useful approach when your business is part of a much larger corporation.

The emphasis on short term operating results has caused some corporate headquarters to treat all business units much the same. Planners have lost sight of strategy and have become score-keepers instead. The short term numbers are all important. This is wrong. Some business units face limited prospects in product development, and few development resources should be allocated here. But others have many opportunities, yet are measured by the same yardstick, and have resources allocated the same way.[16]

It is time to re-introduce a good dose of strategic thinking into your corporate planning exercise. Let's get back to the fundamentals of strategic planning, where differences between businesses and their opportunities were recognized. Recall the BCG (Boston Consulting Group) or McKinsey-GE portfolio model for business units proved very effective when developed in the 1970s.[17] This strategic model was a good one in its day: It plotted all the businesses in the corporation on a two-dimensional grid with "market attractiveness" and "business position" as the axes. Business units were then classified as "stars", "cash cows", "dogs" and "wildcats". The model defined different goals, strategic roles, and even new product emphasis for each business type. This model made a lot of sense at the time, so perhaps it's time to dust it off and update it.

If your business is a "star" business, then it merits an aggressive product innovation effort and more spending on innovation than the average business. A harvest and/or divest strategy is usually elected for "dog" businesses; while "cash cows" see average or modest R&D spending, with product development designed simply to keep the product line up-to-date. And "wildcats", which are the question marks, see selective R&D spending, depending upon the magnitude of the opportunity and track record to date.

One more point about "star" businesses: Be sure to change the performance metrics! Measuring all businesses with the same metrics assumes that all businesses are the same. Again: wrong! For example, your "star" businesses should be treated as "stars" and, most importantly, be measured as "stars". Thus, instead of relying on traditional short term operating profits, apply more growth oriented metrics to gauge their performance, such as:

- Percentage of sales from new products[18]
- Growth in revenue
- Growth in profits.

Note that these growth metrics may not be appropriate for every business unit, just for the designated ones.

Example: At Air Products & Chemicals (a global supplier of industrial gases, equipment and chemicals), each global business unit is assigned its own growth and profitability targets, depending upon each one's type of industry and markets, and the level of importance of the business to the corporation. This approach recognizes that each business unit is different and, as such, should have different targets set for it. Each business unit, thus, has its own New Product Development strategy and corresponding budget that matches its own unique business needs.[19]

2. Investment Based on Objectives and Tasks

This top-down method attempts to ensure that your new product resources are consistent with the tasks needed to achieve your strategy and objectives. Review your product innovation goals and objectives (from Chapter 2). If there are stretch growth objectives, and the strategy is to expand dramatically via new products (typical in a "star" business), then the resources must be in place. For example, since the metric "percentage of revenue from new products" is driven by R&D spending, then new product objectives expressed in terms of sales from new products must be reflected in appropriate levels of R&D spending.[20]

Next, translate your new product sales objectives into new product launches: How many major, medium and minor product launches per year? Then convert these launches over time into resource requirements. How many people and dollars will be required to undertake all the development projects you need to do? This is the demand side, and is usually measured in full-time equivalent people or dollars. Now look at the supply side. Undertake a resource capacity assessment: How many people are available to work on projects? Be sure to subtract the time they must spend on day-to-day work just to keep the business going. This is the supply side.

For more detail on this method, see box insert entitled "Your New Product Objectives – Resource Demand Versus Capacity".[21]

Each time we undertake a resource analysis like this, a gap between demand (based on objectives) and supply is identified. And the result is predicable: The objectives won't be achieved! Senior management, then, has three choices: set more realistic objectives, put the resources in place, or reallocate existing resources. This analysis is an excellent way to decide whether you should be spending more or less on R&D than your current spending levels.

Your New Product Objectives – Resource Demand versus Capacity

Determine resource demand:
- Begin with your new product objectives – what sales or percentage of sales you seek from new products.
- Translate these objectives into numbers of major, medium and minor new product launches annually.
- Determine the number of projects per year you need to move through each stage. (Consider your attrition curve, as in Exhibit 2.8, which shows how many ideas, early stage projects, or development projects it takes to yield one successful launch).
- Next, determine how many person-days required to undertake each stage (broken down by department).
- Calculate the resource demand: The numbers of projects per stage combined with the person-days requirements per project yield the resource demand; namely, the person-days needed to achieve your new product objectives, again by department.

What is your resource capacity?
- Next, look at the capacity available: How many person-days does each department have available for new product project work? (These person-days include all people in that department, and what proportion of their time they have available for new products).

Compare resource demand versus supply:
- Check to see if you have enough resources to achieve your new product objectives.

One outcome of this exercise is determination of the size of the demand-versus-supply resource gap. Another outcome is determination of the ideal resource commitment (or spending level) needed to achieve your product innovation objectives.

3. Investment Based on Competitive Parity

A simpler approach to deciding the correct level of resource commitment to product innovation is by benchmarking your business against others in your industry. This competitive parity approach is based on the premise that the "average competitor" in an industry is close to optimal: Some competitors probably overspend on R&D, and others under spend; but, on balance the average of your industry is just about right.

Currently, average R&D spending in the US is about 3.3 percent of sales. But the big spenders invest a lot more:[22]

Top 10 US firms	8.5 percent of sales on R&D
Top 25 US firms	7.8 percent
Top 100 US firms	5.4 percent
Top 1000 US firms	4.3 percent

The 3.3 percent average figure has remained remarkably constant over the years. On a per-industry basis, the average spending varies widely from a low of 0.4 percent of sales in mature commodity businesses (such as petroleum and coal) to a high of 21.9 percent of sales in fast-paced higher technology industries, such as information software. Exhibit 6.3 provides an industry breakdown so you can compare your business.[23]

If you use this competitive parity approach, there are a few caveats: First, recognize that not all R&D spending goes to new products; some goes to process developments and manufacturing improvements; and some is spent on ongoing technical work required to maintain the product line. Our major benchmarking study revealed that the median spending on R&D is 3.6 percent of sales for companies engaged in product development. Of this R&D spending, the median proportion going to new products is exactly 50 percent, for a median new product spending rate of 1.65 percent of sales.

Second, your product innovation strategy might not parallel the "average competitor's" nor its spending level. Thus, you might decide to spend somewhat more than competitive parity if your strategy is more

Industry	R&D as % of Sales	Industry	R&D as % of Sales
Manufacturing Industries	**3.6**	**Non-manufacturing Industries**	**2.9**
Food	0.7	Mining, extraction and support activities	2.0
Beverage and tobacco products	1.4	Utilities	0.1
Textiles, apparel, leather	1.6	Construction	2.2
Wood products	0.8	Wholesale trade	2.0
Paper, printing, support activities	1.5	Retail trade	0.6
Petroleum and coal products	0.4	Transportation and warehousing	0.4
Chemicals	6.9	Information	5.3
Basic chemicals	2.0	Publishing	17.1
Resin, synthetic rubber, fibers, filament	1.7	Newspaper, periodical, book and database	3.0
Pharmaceuticals and medicines	12.7	Software	21.9
Other chemicals	3.3	Telecommunications	1.0
Plastics and rubber products	1.9	Wired and wireless telecommunications carriers	1.1
Nonmetallic mineral products	1.8	Satellite telecommunications	3.4
Primary metals	0.5	Other telecommunications	0.5
Fabricated metal products	0.8	Internet providers, search portals, data processing	8.7
Machinery	3.6	Internet service providers and search portals	9.0
Computer and electronic products	9.0	Data processing, hosting, related services	8.6
Computers and peripheral equipment	5.4	Other information	0.5
Communications equipment	14.0	Finance, insurance and real estate	0.5
Semiconductor and other electronic components	10.6	Professional, scientific and technical services	10.0
Navigational, electromedical, control instruments	7.0	Architectural, engineering and related services	4.9
Other computer and electronic products	5.6	Computer systems design and related services	9.6
Electrical equipment, appliances and components	2.3	Scientific R&D services	27.4
Transportation equipment	3.0	Other professional, scientific, technical services	3.0
Motor vehicles, trailers and parts	2.5	Health care services	3.9
Aerospace products and parts	4.8	Other non-manufacturing	2.7
Other transportation equipment	1.6		
Furniture and related products	0.8	**All Industries**	**3.3**
Miscellaneous manufacturing	6.1		
Medical equipment and supplies	7.7		
Other miscellaneous manufacturing	2.7		

EXHIBIT 6.3: R&D spending as a percentage of revenue for various industries – both manufacturing and non-manufacturing.[23]

aggressive than the average competitor – for example, being the industry innovator; or somewhat less than the average, if you elect a follower or low-cost strategy.

Example: The annual report of one firm in the instrument industry boasted that the company's strategy is to "be a leader in the field of product innovation in its industry." A closer look at actual spending on R&D showed that the company spent about half the industry average as a percentage of sales. Clearly, there was a strong disconnect between stated strategy and spending level.

Finally, note that while most companies measure and report R&D spending, there are certainly resources other than just R&D required to develop new products. These "other resources" include marketing, sales and operations people, time and expenses; also capital costs, for example, for new equipment. One study estimates that for every dollar you spend on the technical (or R&D) side for new products, you spend two dollars on "other functional areas".[24]

4. Investment Based on Demand Created by New Product Opportunities

The final approach is that your investment level should be determined by the demand in your development pipeline. This is a bottom-up approach (rather than top-down and strategically driven) and it is need-and-opportunity based. The argument here is that development projects are proposed assessed and screened. Thus they are likely solid investment opportunities. Therefore, the resource demands created by approved projects – namely the active and on-hold development projects in your pipeline – is a good gauge of what resources you should devote to product development. For example, if many excellent projects are on-hold awaiting resources, this signals a needed increase in overall resource commitments: you're probably sub-optimizing, not spending enough on product innovation, and letting too many opportunities lie unexploited!

This demand-based exercise is similar to the resource demand-versus-capacity analysis introduced above in approach number 2, except the analysis here is based on resource demands of active and on-hold projects in your development pipeline (rather than the projects needed to achieve your strategic goals).[25] This approach poses the question: Do you have enough of the right resources to handle projects currently in your pipeline? And what about proposed projects that are on-hold due to a lack of resources? The analysis attempts to quantify your projects' demand for resources (usually people, expressed as person-days of work) versus the availability of these resources.

You will likely learn several things from this exercise. First, if you are typical, you have far too many projects in your development pipeline, often by a factor of two or three. And many are "weak" and low-value projects, signaling that it's time to prune the portfolio.[26] Next, you can spot the departments that are the bottlenecks. Finally, you realize that you simply are under-resourced and should devote more resources to product innovation (or alternatively must sub-optimize and put some very attractive projects on hold).

Deploying Your Development Resources: Strategic Portfolio Management

Strategy and new product resource allocation must be intimately connected. And the link is Portfolio Management. Remember: Strategy becomes real when you start spending money! Until you begin allocating resources to specific activities – for example, to specific development areas or to major initiatives – strategy is just words in a document.

Make Shrewd Investment Decisions

There is no direct relationship between R&D spending and significant macro-measures of corporate success such as growth, profitability, and shareholder return, according to a global innovation study of the world's top 1,000 corporate R&D spenders.[27] But while spending more doesn't necessarily help, note that spending too little will hurt. Companies in the bottom 10 percent of R&D spending as a percentage of sales under-perform competitors on gross margins, gross profit, operating profit, and total shareholder returns. Furthermore, there is a strong connection between R&D spending and percentage of sales coming from new products, which is the most popular new product performance metric: The R&D spending devoted to new products is the single strongest driver of the impact of your total new product effort.[28]

In product innovation, money alone doesn't necessarily buy results.[29] Spending level is important, but how you spend the money is equally important. Superior results seem to be a function of the quality of an organization's innovation process – the bets it makes (Portfolio Management) and how it pursues them (Idea-to-Launch System), rather than either the absolute or relative magnitude of its innovation spending. For example, Apple's R&D spending is only 5.9 percent, and trails the computer industry average of 7.6 percent. But by rigorously focusing its development resources on a short list of projects with the greatest potential, the company created an innovation machine that eventually produced the iMac, iBook, iPod, iTunes and iPhone.

What is Portfolio Management?

Portfolio Management is about making these shrewd new product investment decisions. That is, where should the business spend its product innovation resources? Which new product and development projects from the many opportunities the business faces shall it fund? And which ones will receive top priority and be accelerated to market? Portfolio Management is also about business strategy, for today's new product projects decide tomorrow's product-market profile of the firm. Finally, it's about balance: about the optimal investment mix between risk versus return, maintenance versus growth, and short-term versus long-term new product projects.[30]

Strategic Versus Tactical Portfolio Management

Portfolio Management and resource allocation is a hierarchical process, with two levels of decision making. This hierarchical approach simplifies the decision challenge somewhat (Exhibit 6.4).[31]

- *High level – Strategic Portfolio Management:* Strategic portfolio decisions answer the question: Directionally, where should your business spend its new product resources (people and funds)? How should you split your resources across projects types, markets, technologies or product categories? And on what major initiatives or new platforms should you concentrate your resources? Establishing Strategic Buckets and defining Strategic Product Roadmaps are effective tools which we outline below and in the next chapter.
- *Lower level – Tactical portfolio decisions:* Tactical portfolio decisions focus on individual projects, but obviously follow from the strategic

decisions. They address the question: What specific new product projects should you do? Such decisions are shown at the bottom part of Exhibit 6.4, are tactical, and are not the topic of this book. Many excellent methods for rating and prioritizing projects are available and are outlined in our other articles and books.[32]

This book deals with innovation strategy, so it looks only at strategic or high-level portfolio management decisions – the upper two-thirds of Exhibit 6.4.

The Impact of Portfolio Management on Business Performance

An effective Portfolio Management System is *one of the top best practices in product innovation*. This is one overriding conclusion of our own major benchmarking study.[33] Exhibit 6.5 reveals the results, and here is

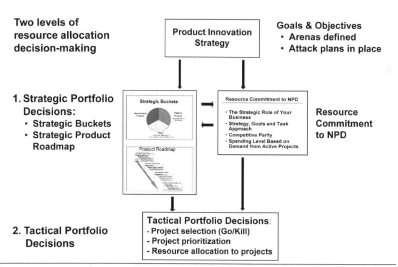

EXHIBIT 6.4: Move from your business's Product Innovation Strategy to Portfolio Management. Portfolio Management and resource allocation is a hierarchical decision process with two levels of decision making.

what the top performing businesses possess that distinguish them from the rest:

1. Top performers have a visible, formal portfolio management decision process in place. This portfolio system is designed to optimally allocate development resources to types of projects and to select the right projects: More than three-quarters of businesses lack a proficient Portfolio Management process. But having such a Portfolio Management system does make a big difference: Top performers are eight times as likely as poor performers to have such a system.

> *Example:* EXFO Engineering boasts a very disciplined project ranking and prioritization "Portfolio Process". Senior management at EXFO rates their approach to Portfolio Management to be the company's strongest best practice and attributes a reduction in time-to-market (from 18-24 months to 12 months) to their portfolio system.[34]
>
> The Portfolio Process session is held quarterly, takes about five days, and is undertaken by a portfolio team comprised of the executives. The session begins with a strategy review, followed by a technology overview. Subsequent steps in the process include the project post-mortem recommendations; a quick review of ongoing projects; and gate review presentations for upcoming or new projects. The portfolio team then undertakes a project prioritization exercise using scorecard criteria. This prioritization exercise parallels EXFO's gating process and enables the portfolio team to kill a project if necessary. Next, the portfolio team performs a final prioritization, but this time with "loadings" (that is, resource requirements per project). The final step in EXFO's portfolio review process is staff feedback.

2. Best performers' portfolios are aligned with the business's objectives and strategy. That is, all the projects in the portfolio fit or support the strategy. This practice is the only positive of the six portfolio practices highlighted in Exhibit 6.5, with the majority of businesses (57.2 percent) achieving strategic alignment. This practice is also a strong discriminator between best and worst performers, and is correlated strongly with new product performance.

3. In top performers, the breakdown of spending in the portfolio truly reflects the business's strategy. This is another practice designed to achieve strategic alignment – ensuring that spending splits across project types, markets, business areas, etc. mirrors the strategic priorities of the business. If there are disconnects between stated business strategy and where the resources are spent, the portfolio is in trouble and strategic alignment is missing. This facet of strategic alignment is a weak area: Only 30.7 percent of businesses claim good alignment between business strategy and resource splits. Again this practice is a significant discriminator between top and poor performers (with only 8.0 percent of poor performers achieving this strategic resource split versus a relative high of 65.5 percent for top performers).

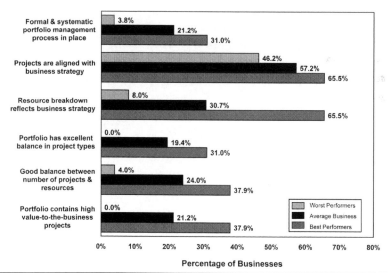

EXHIBIT 6.5: The percentage of businesses utilizing each of six different portfolio management practices is quite low. Most firms are deficient here, but top performers fare better.

Example: MARS Petfoods in Australia has the company's most refined portfolio system globally. Among many views of the portfolio that management sees, there are pie charts that reveal the breakdown of resources on key strategic dimensions. These pie charts include project types (resources broken down by disruptive, progressive, continuous and tactical projects) and also product category (premium health, core dry, health, etc.), and capture current resource commitments to development projects (Exhibit 6.6).[35] The pie charts and their resource breakdowns are then compared to the business strategy and strategic direction. If there are disconnects, corrections are made to the mix of projects at periodic portfolio reviews.

4. Best performers have an excellent balance of projects: long-term versus short-term, high-risk versus low-risk, and across markets and technologies. Here too, most businesses are weak, confessing to unbalanced portfolios

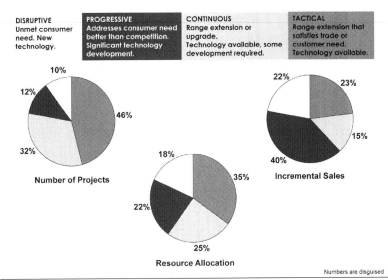

EXHIBIT 6.6: Three different views of a portfolio are shown, broken down by project types. Here the pie charts show the breakdown by numbers of projects, resource split, and by results (as measured by first year incremental sales).[35]

of projects, with only 19.4 percent having well-balanced portfolios. Note that top performers again fare moderately well here, while not one poor performing business achieves the right balance. This is the second most strongly correlated portfolio practice with innovation performance in Exhibit 6.5.

> *Example:* Bausch & Lomb balances its portfolio by controlling the mix of short, medium and long term projects. Currently about one-third of its projects are expected to launch within two years; half in three to four years; and the remainder farther out. The goal is to launch a new product every quarter. This split allows the portfolio team to judge balance in the portfolio, assessing whether it is too short-term focused.

5. Top performers strike a good balance between the number of new projects undertaken and the resources available: The goal is to balance resource availabilities (people, time and money) with resource demand (the number of projects), and not to do more projects at a time than can be handled effectively. But this is a very weak practice in Portfolio Management: Only 24 percent of businesses achieve this resource project balance. Again top performers do much better, with 37.9 percent achieving resource balance (versus only 4.0 percent of poor performers).

> *Example:* EXFO Engineering undertakes periodic portfolio reviews four times per year as one way to ensure the right balance between resource availability and demand. EXFO ranks its projects – best to worst – noting resource demands or "loadings" (person-days) for each one. When the resource demand exceeds the supply, a line is drawn: All projects below the line are put on hold.

6. Best performers' portfolios contain high value new product projects – profitable, high return projects with solid commercial prospects. Picking the winners – the high value-to-the-business projects – is no easy task. And only a small minority of businesses (21.2 percent) claim to have achieved this ability to load their portfolios with high value projects. Top performers fare better here, with 37.9 percent having high value projects in their portfolios versus zero percent for poor performers. Seeking high value projects is the most strongly correlated with performance of all the practices listed in Exhibit 6.5.

> *Example:* Air Products & Chemicals achieves positive results by using a standardized project impact analysis across all projects. Each project is assessed using a leverage-profitability index, which is determined by dividing the project's NPV by its cost. This leverage-profitability index is then used to compare all projects against each other and to prioritize them. Air Product's goal is to see the day where new product development teams will perform their own impact analyses, and compare projects across platforms based on their total projected expectations. In this way, the value of the portfolio will be maximized.

Using Strategic Buckets to Drive the Right Mix and Balance of Projects

A major challenge most managements face in product innovation is: Strategically, where should your business spend its resources when it comes to product innovation – on what types of projects, and in what product, market or technology areas? And how much do you wish to spend in each area? Note, if senior management does not make this decision, it will be made for them… by way of a number of smaller, ad hoc decisions made during the year. The trouble is, the default option is almost always wrong!

The Strategic Buckets model operates from the simple principle that implementing strategy equates to spending money on specific projects. Thus, operationalizing your strategy really means "setting spending targets".

The method begins with the business's strategy, and requires senior management to make forced choices along each of several key dimensions – choices about how they wish to allocate their scarce resources. This enables the creation of "envelopes of resources" or "buckets". Existing projects are then categorized into buckets and one determines whether actual spending is consistent with desired spending for each bucket. Finally, projects are prioritized within buckets to arrive at the ultimate portfolio of projects – ones that mirrors management's strategy for the business.

Example: A rather simple breakdown is used at Honeywell: their "Mercedes Benz star" method of allocating resources (Exhibit 6.7). The leadership team begins with the business strategy, and uses the three-slice pie chart to help divide up the resources. There are three buckets:

- Fundamental research and platform development projects (which promise to yield major breakthroughs and new technology platforms)
- New product developments
- Maintenance (technical support, product improvements, cost reductions, product enhancements, etc.).

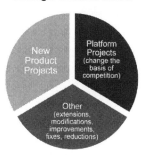

Honeywell's 'Mercedes Star' Strategic Buckets Model

- Management makes strategic choices in terms of:
  - Project types
  - Market segments
  - Product lines or
  - Technologies
- Projects are categorized into Buckets
- Projects are ranked in each Bucket until out of resources
  - Use different ranking criteria per Bucket
- Resource allocation thus mirrors strategic priorities

EXHIBIT 6.7: Use the Strategic Buckets method to translate strategy Into strategic portfolio decisions. The business's strategy dictates the split of resources into buckets.

Management allocates its R&D funds across these three buckets. Next, the projects are sorted into each of the three buckets. Management then ranks projects against each other within each bucket. In effect, three separate portfolios of projects are created and managed. And the spending breakdowns across buckets and project types mirror strategic priorities.

Determining the Size of the Buckets

It sounds simple in theory. But how does one decide the size of these Strategic Buckets in the first place? Typically, management employs a modified- or mini-Delphi process. The meeting begins with a review of the strategy for the business and for each of the major product lines or market segments, including the product innovation strategy and goals. Next is the current-state assessment which consists of:

- A historical review – where the money was spent for the last few years (typically a review of pie chart splits across markets, business areas, project types and perhaps geographies, much like the MARS Petfoods example above).
- An assessment of the productivity of past R&D spending. For example, what has been the yield or productivity from spending on different types of projects, or across different business sectors? An example is shown in Exhibit 6.8 from Ivoclar Vivadent, a Swiss dental devices company. (If productivities are not known, then at least undertake a historical results analysis of major projects).
- A review of the current split in resources, again using the same types of pie charts.
- A quick review of major projects underway, including their prospects and resource commitments to these initiatives.
- A look at the resource splits for best-in-class companies. (Exhibit 6.9 for sample data).

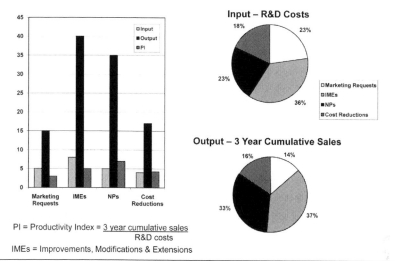

PI = Productivity Index = $\dfrac{\text{3 year cumulative sales}}{\text{R\&D costs}}$

IMEs = Improvements, Modifications & Extensions

EXHIBIT 6.8: How productive your spending has been in the past helps to decide the size of Strategic Buckets. The example above shows productivities by project types. Here, New Products fare the best.

	Worst Performers	Average Business	Best Performers
Promotional Developments & Package Changes	12%	10%	6%
Incremental Product Improvements & Changes	40%	33%	28%
Major Product Revisions	19%	22%	25%
New To The Business Products	20%	24%	24%
New To The World Products	7%	10%	16%
	~45%	~55%	~65%

├──────── **10 Point Steps** ────────┤

Note: columns do not add up to 100% due to a small percentage of "other" projects.

EXHIBIT 6.9: In making your Strategic Buckets decisions, be sure to consider the portfolios of best-in-class companies. Best performers focus more on innovative and game-changing projects.

These are the inputs to the decision-making meeting, as highlighted in Exhibit 6.10. Next comes the Delphi voting, where each senior manager simply writes down what they believe the correct split of resources should be across several different dimensions.

Example: At a major tool manufacturer, one dozen key executives take part in the Strategic Buckets annual meeting. The current splits in resources, along with a list of current major projects, is presented. So are the overall business strategy and the strategies for each of the firm's four major product lines. Then the executives vote by allocating resources as percentages across product lines, across project types, and across geographic regions of the world. These votes are immediately displayed on a large screen utilizing an Excel spreadsheet, are debated, and consensus is reached. The buckets are decided.

In another company, each executive is given 100 poker chips along with a "game board" which shows various categories of projects and business areas. They make the necessary splits into buckets by placing the poker chips on the areas of the game board. It is a very visual and effective method.

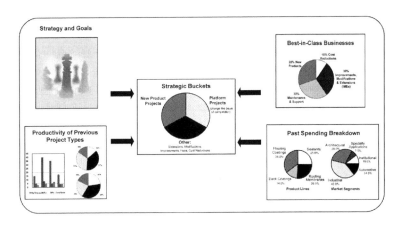

EXHIBIT 6.10: There are many inputs or factors to consider in deciding on the size of your Strategic Buckets. Include a summary or review of these at your Strategic Buckets decision meeting.

Dimensions to Use for the Buckets

What dimensions should be used in the Strategic Buckets splits? One leading R&D planning executive explained: "Whatever dimensions the leadership team of the business find most relevant to describe their own strategy". In other businesses, such as ITT Industries, the dimensions used in each business unit are prescribed; ITT uses two dimensions, namely project types and business areas. Honeywell uses project types as in Exhibits 6.6 and 6.7, plus other dimensions that are relevant to each business unit. A typical three-dimensional split, used by a major US chemical company, is shown in Exhibit 6.11.

Some common dimensions that you might consider are listed in Exhibit 6.12 in order of popularity, and include:

- *Strategic Arenas:* The most obvious spending split is across the strategic arenas just defined and prioritized in Chapter 4. That is, having assessed the attractiveness of each arena in Exhibits 4.11 and

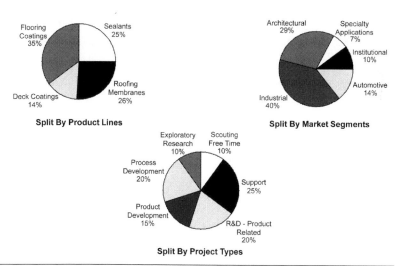

EXHIBIT 6.11: This sample Strategic Buckets decision from a major chemical company uses three dimensions: product lines, market segments, and project types. Use two or three dimensions for Strategic Buckets.

4.12 and defined the priorities of each, move to deployment – deciding how many resources each arena or battlefield should receive.

- *Strategic goals:* Management splits resources across the specified strategic goals. For example, what percent should be spent on Defending the Base? On Diversifying? On Extending the Base?
- *Markets and segments:* Splitting resources by markets is the most popular approach (an example is in Exhibit 6.11). Markets are often closely related to strategic arenas, above.
- *Product lines:* Resources are split across product lines: For example, how much to spend on Product Line A? On Product Line B? On C? A plot of product life-cycle curves coupled with a review of strategic opportunities for each product line helps determine this split.
- *Types of projects:* Decisions or splits can be made in terms of types of projects (as in Exhibit 6.7). The majority of firms use a breakdown by project types, simply because most managements fear that they do, indeed, have too many of the wrong types of projects.

> *Example:* Given its aggressive product innovation stance, EXFO Engineering's management targets 65 percent of R&D spending to genuine new products; another 10 percent to platform developments and research (technology development for the future); and the final 25 percent goes to incrementals (the "support-folio", namely product modifications, fixes and improvements).[36]

- *Technologies or technology platforms:* Spending splits can be made across technology types (e.g., base, key, pacing and embryonic technologies) or across specific technology platforms (Platforms X, Y and Z).
- *Familiarity matrix:* This is the split of resources into different types of markets and to different technology types in terms of their familiarity to the business. You can use the popular "familiarity matrix" – technology newness versus market newness – to help split

resources (similar to Exhibit 4.1 in Chapter 4) although with nine cells, this may prove to be too fine a split).[37]

- *Geography:* What proportion of resources should be spent on projects aimed largely at North America? At Latin America? At Europe? At Asia-Pacific? Or on global projects?
- *Stage of development:* Some businesses distinguish between early stage projects and projects in development and beyond. Two buckets are created, one for development projects, the other for early stage projects. One division at GTE allocates "seed corn money" to a separate bucket for early stage projects.

Most firms use a maximum of three dimensions from the above list for their strategic buckets (more than that, and the decision process becomes quite cumbersome – too many pie charts). These bucket allocation decisions, thus, yield a strategic and ideal split of resources on relevant dimensions to the business – the targets or "what should be".

Popularity	Dimension	Buckets (examples)
1	Market	Markets, segments, sectors or geography
2	Project Types	Platforms, new products, maintenance, improvements, cost reductions
3	Product Line	For commercial banks: deposits, loans, info products, FX, payroll
4	Project Size	Major/minor; by $000 expenditure
5	Technology	Embryonic/pacing/base; or by technology type or area
6	Platform	Platform types – for cell phones: speaker, battery, display, keypad
7	Strategic Goals	Against specific strategies: defend base; extend base; diversify business

EXHIBIT 6.12: These are the typical dimensions used for Strategic Buckets.

Gap Analysis – Adding Up the Projects

Following this splitting or voting exercise comes a gap analysis. Exhibit 6.13 shows an example with four Buckets, each with its spending limit already decided. Existing, proposed and on-hold projects are now categorized by bucket, and projects within each Bucket are rank-ordered. You can use either financial criteria or a scoring model to do this ranking within Buckets.[38] For two of the Buckets in Exhibit 6.13 – new products and salesforce requests – two different scorecards are used that capture the relative attractiveness of projects; for the other two buckets – cost reductions and product improvements – a financial metric, a type of productivity index, is used to rank projects.

Next, the total spend by bucket is added up – the "what would be" if all the projects were undertaken in that bucket. Spending gaps are then identified between the strategically-determined "what should be" and "what would be" for each bucket. Note that if all the projects are

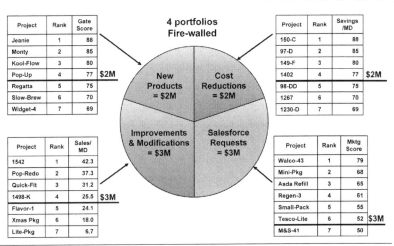

Project	Rank	Gate Score
Jeanie	1	88
Monty	2	85
Kool-Flow	3	80
Pop-Up	4	77
Regatta	5	75
Slow-Brew	6	70
Widget-4	7	69

$2M

Project	Rank	Savings /MD
150-C	1	88
97-D	2	85
149-F	3	80
1402	4	77
98-DD	5	75
1267	6	70
1230-D	7	69

$2M

4 portfolios Fire-walled

New Products = $2M
Cost Reductions = $2M
Improvements & Modifications = $3M
Salesforce Requests = $3M

Project	Rank	Sales/ MD
1542	1	42.3
Pop-Redo	2	37.3
Quick-Fit	3	31.2
1498-K	4	25.5
Flavor-1	5	24.1
Xmas Pkg	6	18.0
Lite-Pkg	7	6.7

$3M

Project	Rank	Mktg Score
Walco-43	1	79
Mini-Pkg	2	68
Asda Refill	3	65
Regen-3	4	61
Small-Pack	5	55
Tesco-Lite	6	52
M&S-41	7	50

$3M

EXHIBIT 6.13: Four Strategic Buckets (different project types) are used, with projects categorized into each bucket. Rank projects and list them until out of resources in that bucket. Use different ranking criteria per bucket.

approved in Exhibit 6.13, then all four Buckets are overspent (the cut-off line shows where the resource limits are reached). Portfolio adjustments are then made, either via immediate pruning of projects, or by toughening up (or relaxing) the approval process for future projects.

The Right Split in Project Types

A major strategic question is: What is the best mix or balance of development projects – for example, incremental developments versus true innovations? Certainly, a business's new product strategy should ideally be reflected in the breakdown of types of product developments it undertakes – where the funds are invested. Additionally, breakdowns of new products and projects by type are a predictor of product innovation performance. For example, too much emphasis on short term, small projects might point to an under-achieving business. Exhibit 6.9 shows breakdown results from our major benchmarking study. You can evaluate your own business against this:

- Incremental product improvement and changes is the dominant category, representing 33 percent of all projects in the average business
- Next are new products to the business, accounting for 24 percent
- Then come major product revisions, making up 22 percent of projects.

What we witness is a fairly even balance among projects across these three most popular categories. Note that on average, non-innovative products – incrementals, revisions and promotional developments – together account for about 65 percent of projects. By contrast, new-to-the-world products – true innovations – represent a minority of development projects at only 10 percent.

Do the top performing firms adopt a particular mix of project types? Does an optimal portfolio of project types exist? Consider how the average business compares to the best and worst performing businesses in

Exhibit 6.9. What is noteworthy is the shift towards much more innovative and bolder projects as one moves from worst to best performers. For example, considering only the bottom three categories – major revisions, new-to-the-business and new-to-the-world – there is roughly a 10-point step change across the chart from worst performers to best performers. As in the stock market, choosing the right balance and mix in your portfolio really does pay off!

The argument is not that businesses should only undertake true innovations and genuine new products. Product improvements and modifications are certainly needed to keep a product line healthy and to respond to customer requests. But when these incremental projects dominate your portfolio, take care – you're starting to look a lot like a poor performing company.

The Power of Strategic Buckets

The major strength of the Strategic Buckets approach is that it firmly links your new product spending to your business strategy. One helpful rule is not to move resources from one Bucket to another. Thus, over time, and when applied with discipline, the portfolio of projects and the spending across Strategic Buckets will equal management's desired spending targets. Strategic alignment will be achieved as resource commitments truly mirror strategic priorities.

Another positive facet of Strategic Buckets is the recognition that all development projects that compete for the same resources should be considered. Note that new products are not the only bucket in Exhibit 6.13; cost reductions and salesforce requests, which use many of the same resources as new products, are also part of the bucketing exercise.

By taking this approach companies are not faced with comparing and ranking diverse types of projects against each other; for example, comparing major new product projects to minor modifications. This is because only products within the same bucket are compared; new products against other new products; platforms against other platforms – but not across Buckets. Further, different rating or ranking criteria are used for each type of project, as in Exhibit 6.13. (Without this differentiated ranking, when major and venturesome projects are compared against the smaller lower risk ones, invariably the latter will win. This is one reason why most firms have an overabundance of low value, low-hanging fruit projects.) Finally, because Strategic Buckets is a two-step approach – first allocate money to buckets, and then prioritize similar projects within Buckets – it is not necessary to arrive at a universal set of scoring or ranking criteria that fits all projects.

Example: In Chempro's case (from the last few chapters), management prioritizes four new Strategic Arenas, along with the existing arena, namely home-base. The arena map in Exhibit 4.12 provides a good guide for this prioritization exercise. Also considered are new product opportunities or possible projects that are proposed within each arena. After much discussion and analysis, spending levels are established for each one (Exhibit 6.14 for Chempro's deployments).

Additionally, Chempro's management develops Strategic Buckets by project type: genuine new products, product improvements and cost

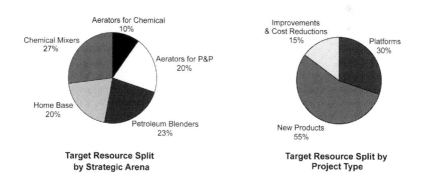

Target Resource Split by Strategic Arena

Target Resource Split by Project Type

EXHIBIT 6.14: Chempro's management employs two dimensions for Strategic Buckets: arenas (defined by products and markets) and project types. Management 'votes' on how much to spend in each Bucket.

reductions and platform developments (Exhibit 6.14). Here, the arenas chosen and the nature of the developments required in each arena help to decide the resource split by project types.

Strategic Buckets – Wrap-Up

Strategic Buckets is a simple concept, but it has profound implications to the way you manage your portfolio decisions. Instead of just letting the portfolio be decided by the projects you select, you've reversed the order – letting strategy decide what the mix and balance in the portfolio should be. It is similar to the difference between an amateur investor who buys stocks one at a time and a professional portfolio manager, who first decides the strategic breakdown of the portfolio – stocks, bonds, and property – and then makes specific investment decisions. This chapter has outlined a proven method for developing your Strategic Buckets, along with a number of practical examples to show how the method works. Strategic Buckets are a logical tool for translating your product innovation strategy into reality. So give Strategic Buckets a try – it's a powerful tool for getting from concept to action.

CHAPTER 7

Your Strategic Roadmaps

Strategy without tactics is the slowest route to victory.

Sun Tzŭ, c. 490 BC

What is a Roadmap?

Strategic planning is a business process that combines market and industry analysis with the necessary capabilities and competencies required to fulfill customer needs in that market. Roadmapping has emerged as an effective way of creating and visualizing the resulting strategy and its elements. Strategic Roadmapping provides a bridge among all the strategic and tactical decision processes, business functions, and organizational units though the common element of time.[1]

A roadmap is simply management's view of how to get where they want to go or to achieve their desired objective.[2] The Strategic Roadmap is a useful tool that helps senior management visualize what major initiatives will be executed over time, and it helps to ensure that the capabilities to achieve their objective are in place when needed.

In the context of product innovation, roadmapping defines the plan for the evolution of your products; it links your innovation strategy to your plans for new products and to the technologies needed to develop them.[3] Roadmapping helps to identify, select, sequence and prioritize a set of major product development initiatives, and it provides a way to develop, organize and present information on:

- What new products or product lines your business will develop
- What new product platforms you will develop to support these product developments
- The timing and sequence of these developments
- And even the technologies to be invested in, either through internal technology development work or technology acquisition and licensing-in.

The resulting product roadmap sets "placemarks" for development projects into the future; that is, an ear-marking of resources or a tentative commitment to projects.

Strategic Roadmapping is a multi-faceted, cross-functional product planning process, requiring many strategic, tactical and other inputs. It is a strategically-driven resource allocation method, and can be used instead of, or along with, the Strategic Buckets approach in the last chapter. This top-down approach is designed to ensure that the proposed development projects contribute to, or are essential for, the realization of your business's strategy and goals.[4] A Strategic Product Roadmap is an effective way to map out this series of initiatives in an attack plan.

Note that there are different types of roadmaps: the strategic product roadmap which lays out the sequence of major product developments and their timing; and the technology roadmap (also strategic), which maps what technologies will be required and when. This chapter reveals methods for developing both types of roadmaps, as they are closely linked.

From Strategy to Roadmaps

Let's use a military analogy: You are a five-star General at war. You have clearly specified goals – presumably to win the war or to achieve certain ends. You have identified certain key strategic arenas – fronts or major battlefields – on a map where you plan to attack and win. But as you chart your strategy, you see that there are some assaults or initiatives you will have to engage in along the way – individual battles that you must fight in order to see your strategy succeed.

Now let's translate the elements of the General's strategy to a Strategic Roadmapping context for product innovation:

- *Goals and objectives:* What product innovation goals and objectives your business has; for example, what percentage of your business's growth over the next three years will come from new products? Goals and objectives are the topic of Chapter 2.
- *Arenas, fronts and major battlefields:* These are the strategic arenas defined in your business and new product strategy (in Chapters 3 and 4). That is, which markets, technologies and product types do you plan to attack? Where will you focus your new product efforts?
- *Attack plans:* How do you plan to win on each battlefield or arena? Will you launch a frontal assault (be the innovator and first in), or adopt a more conservative, wait-see-and-attack strategy (fast follower)? Will you attack with a global plan, or perhaps a "glocal" or local one? Finally, will you attack alone or try to form an alliance, and venture into the arena with a partner. Attack plans are the topic of Chapter 5.
- *Deployment:* How many troops do you deploy to each battlefield, front or strategic arena? Making the right resource commitments and defining strategic buckets are key to the resource issue and are the topics of Chapter 6.
- *Assaults and initiatives:* These are the major developments that you must undertake in order to implement your strategy – the major new product, technology or platform developments: your Strategic Roadmap – the topic of this chapter.

Tactical Versus Strategic Roadmaps

Our focus in this chapter is on *Strategic Roadmaps,* as opposed to Tactical Roadmaps. A Strategic Roadmap lays out only the major and strategic development initiatives, including major new products and technology developments. It is longer term, and can be for as long as five or seven years forward.

By comparison, a *Tactical Roadmap* provides more detail, and is a precise outline of each and every product release, extension, improvement or modification. It is often for one product group or line, and often developed by the product manager. Usually this roadmap also contains details on the nature, attributes and performance characteristics of the products in the map. It tends to be more short term, for example, one year.

A five-to-seven year time-frame may seem like a long time, and extremely difficult to forecast and plan for. It is! But note that a Strategic Product Roadmap is an evolving or "evergreen" plan. Because it is updated annually (or even more frequently), only the first year is implemented as is. Roadmaps are not static plans, but rather are snapshots of a rolling strategy at any point in time.[5]

The Objectives of Roadmapping

The overall goal of roadmapping usually is to create dynamic, long-term integrated plans for product and technology development. When employing roadmapping, you should have at least three objectives in mind:

1. Assess the uncertainties of the long-term future in a systematic and methodical manner.
2. Move beyond assessment to develop planned responses to evolving market needs, customer requirements, competitor threats and regulatory changes.
3. Understand and dynamically align your technology development and investment plans, product development efforts, market needs, and high-level company strategies as they evolve and change over time.

Types of Maps

Product Roadmaps

Your Strategic Product Roadmap defines your major new product and product-platform developments along a timeline. An example is Exhibit 7.1 for Chempro. Here the product roadmap not only sets out the major product introductions and their timing, it also defines the platforms and platform extensions needed to develop these new products.

> *Example:* Recall that Chemo identified four arenas, besides home-base, as areas of focus, shown in Chapter 4, Exhibit 4.12:
> * Aerators for the chemical industry (waste water treatment)
> * Blenders for the petroleum industry
> * Agitators and mixers for the chemical industry
> * Surface aerators for the pulp and paper industry.
> Although these are adjacent arenas to the current business, clearly the company does not have sufficient resources to undertake all four concurrently. So a Strategic Roadmap is crafted.
>
> The first major initiative or attack is "mixers for the chemical industry" (the first box). This is an easy move, as it is an adjacent arena, and can be done using the company's existing product platform. Three new products – basic mixers, specialty impellers and then high power mixers – are envisioned in Exhibit 7.1, and mapped out over a 24 month period.
>
> Next, beginning in about one year, a second platform extension is planned, this time into "petroleum mixers" (second box), another attractive and adjacent area. And two development programs are planned: a low-power product line, and later a higher-power line of mixers. This initiative or arena attack takes Chempro three years into the future.
>
> There are no further attractive arenas that can be attacked with merely a platform extension. So a new platform – for surface aerators

(waste water aeration and treatment) – must be developed. But note that management wisely elects its home-base market, namely the current pulp-and-paper industry sector, as the first market to attack (third box). These new aerator products are desired starting in year four, so the platform development must get underway in about 25 months (and after the first initiative above is completed). Three development programs are planned in order to yield three aerator product lines for pulp-and-paper waste water treatment.

Finally, this aerator platform will be extended in yet another attractive arena, "aerators for chemical waste" (the last box), which is synergistic with the first initiative above, "chemical mixers".

What happened? Did the company follow this roadmap exactly? No, not quite, but the roadmap in Exhibit 7.1 did provide a solid initial plan and good direction. Some of the new product projects originally envisioned in Exhibit 7.1, upon further investigation, proved unattractive, so they were killed and replaced with others. The timeline

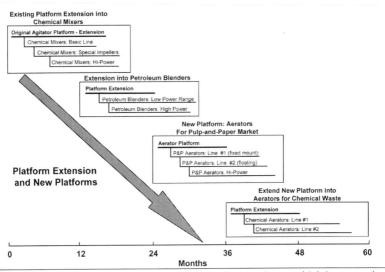

EXHIBIT 7.1: Chempro develops its strategic product roadmap, which lays out the major new product and new product platform initiatives over the next five years. Note this is an evolving or "rolling" plan.

proved a bit ambitious, and took longer to implement than the five years. But the four Strategic Arenas remained, as did the aerator platform development. Ultimately, products were launched with success in all four arenas, the result of a solid innovation strategy and proficient execution.

Most often, the specification of development projects in your Strategic Product Roadmap is left fairly general and high-level. Designations such as "a low carb beer for the Atkins diet market," or "ceramic coated drill bits for the aerospace industry," or "low power petroleum blenders," as in Exhibit 7.1 are often the way these projects are shown on the product roadmap. Placemarks for projects yet to be defined are the norm. The product roadmap is meant to be directional and strategic, but not to provide detailed product and project definitions. As each project progresses through the idea-to-launch process, however, the project and product becomes increasingly specified and defined.

Technology Roadmaps

The *Technology Roadmap* is derived from the product roadmap, and specifies technologically how you will get there. That is, it lays out the technologies and technological competencies that are needed in order to implement (develop and source) the products and platforms in your product roadmap. The technology roadmap is a logical extension of the product roadmap and is closely linked to it. Indeed, at Lucent Technologies, the two are combined into a product-technology roadmap as a tool to help management link business strategy, product plans and technology development.[6]

Platforms: A Base from Which to Operate

Many businesses now look to platforms as a way to think about strategic thrusts in product development. And the term "platform" is often heard in roadmapping discussions. For example, in the Chempro roadmap

(Exhibit 7.1), the terms "new platform" and "platform extension" are used. The problem is, like many words in business, the term "platform" has evolved to have different meanings in different industries and contexts.

The original notion of a platform was very much product based. For example, the PDMA handbook defines a product platform as the "design and components that are shared by a set of products in a product family. From this platform, numerous derivatives can be designed".[7] Thus Chrysler's engine-transmission for its 1970s K-car was a platform that spawned other vehicles over the years, including the Chrysler minivan.

The notion of platforms has since been broadened to include technological capabilities. For example, ExxonMobil's metallocene platform is simply a catalyst and related polymerization technology that has yielded an entirely new generation of polymers. So a platform is like an oil drilling platform in the ocean in which you invest heavily. From this platform, you can drill many holes relatively quickly and at low cost.

In the field of product innovation, the platform establishes the capability; and, this capability spawns many new product projects much more quickly and cost effectively than starting from scratch each time. Examples of platforms are: a deposit software platform in a bank, from which many end-user deposit products can be developed; or, a printer-head assembly from which multiple models of computer printers are built.

The definition of platforms has also been broadened to include marketing or branding concepts as well as technological capabilities. For example, some consider 3M's *Post-It Notes* to be a marketing platform, which has created many individual products. General Mills' *Old El Paso* products – a line of Tex-Mex ingredients and complete meals – is another example of a marketing platform.

New and existing platforms are often defined in the Strategic Product (or technology) Roadmap. For example, having identified certain markets as Strategic Arenas, certain new product-platforms or technology-platforms may be required in order to win in these market arenas.

Example: Recall Chempro's product roadmap in Exhibit 7.1. Note that this roadmap outlines not only the major new product projects to be developed, but also the new product platforms, and their timing needed to successfully attack the designated Strategic Arenas.[8] For example, top priority is given to extension of the current platform – agitators and mixers – to both the chemical and petroleum industries. A new platform is envisioned as the next major initiative after extension possibilities are exhausted.

Roadmaps as Forecasts

Some roadmappers use the term "roadmap" to denote an industry forecast. For example, a "technology roadmap" is sometimes used to show the expected evolution of technologies in an industry, and the performance various technologies will achieve over time. An "environmental roadmap" shows what will happen in the external environment.

Strictly speaking, these are not roadmaps, but forecasts. Note that a roadmap is defined as a time-based map of major development initiatives that the business will undertake to achieve its objectives. To avoid confusion, we use the term "forecast" to denote a prediction of what will occur in an industry, market or technology, and "roadmap" to denote a map of the major development initiatives your business expects to undertake over time.

The Logical Sequence of Maps

Strategic Roadmapping begins with an understanding of the external competitive and market environment, the "know why" at the top of Exhibit 7.2. Much of this analysis and forecasting is the topic of Chapter 3.

Next comes the product roadmap or the "know what" in Exhibit 7.2. It maps the planned products to be offered and when. In some product roadmaps, the specification of expected product differentiation and product attributes is part of the roadmap, although this level of detail may be too much for a strategic, longer term roadmap.

EXHIBIT 7.2: Roadmapping begins with a strategic analysis, leading to the product roadmap. The technology roadmap flows from the product roadmap, and ultimately results in the action plan.

The technology roadmap follows, which deals with the "know how" issue. It lays out the technologies needed to develop the products in the product roadmap and, in more detailed versions, links those technologies to specific product attributes or performance characteristics.

The action plan or "to do" follows. It specifies resources required to accomplish the various roadmaps, and the next steps. The business's Stage-Gate process usually is the tactical tool to implement the product development and technology development programs .[9,10]

The linkages among the various maps are shown in Exhibit 7.3.[11] The map begins on the left with "where are we now". Then note "where do we want to be" on the far right, which is the objective of the mapping exercise. And in the middle are the items under the heading "how do we get there". The vital time dimension is shown from left to right, across the maps. Note that specific components of each map – for example, major market trends, or R&D projects, or resources required – should also be shown on the map, with the linkages drawn as arrows. Strong links – for example, drivers or dependencies – are shown in bold.

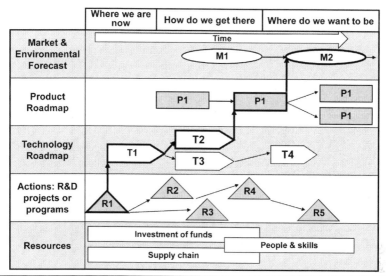

EXHIBIT 7.3: Move from forecasts to roadmaps. Show the linkages among projects. Move from 'where we are now' to 'where we want to be'.[11]

Example: A set of roadmaps is illustrated for a firm in the aircraft industry in Exhibit 7.4 (adapted, with data disguised). Note how the mapping begins with a market and industry trends analysis, showing trends for both airline customers and the airlines, along with environmental trends (top section across diagram in Exhibit 7.4).

The middle section shows the envisioned product roadmap – what the aircraft company must or will likely offer over time in terms of new products. These are broken down by category: new product and service offerings, new engines, new materials and new aircraft performance. The bottom section shows the technologies that will be required to deliver these products with the required performance: engines, materials, systems.

As in the previous chart (Exhibit 7.3), the linkages between elements or components in this aircraft manufacturer's map – what drives what, or what is needed – should be shown, with key linkages identified.

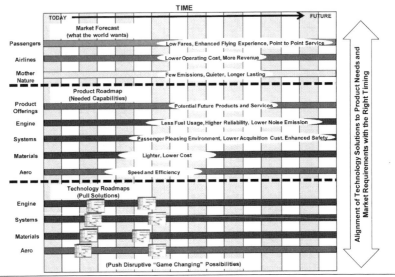

EXHIBIT 7.4: Here is an example of how the market forecast drives the product roadmap, which in turn drives the technology roadmap — adapted from a firm in the aircraft industry.

Developing Your Strategic Product Roadmap

There is no easy formula for roadmapping. It is strategic, multi-faceted and has many inputs. Roadmapping requires a cross-functional team of experts – we'll call this team the "roadmapping task-force" – who meet to develop a framework for organizing and presenting the critical product-planning information.

Exhibit 7.5 shows the many inputs to developing a product roadmap. Some of these inputs were part of the market, industry and technology analysis done in Chapter 3. Recall that Chapter 3's analysis tries to identify Strategic Arenas and adjacencies where your business might focus new product efforts. In developing a roadmap, you revisit these analyses, but with a somewhat different purpose; this time to try to identify specific new products that your business should or could develop. So let's look at these analyses from Chapter 3 quickly, and your arena selection exercise in

Chapter 4, to see how both are used as inputs to the creation of your Strategic Product Roadmap (and your Technology Roadmap).

1. Translate Your Innovation Strategy Directly Into Strategic Initiatives

The development of your product roadmap flows logically from your product innovation strategy. Thus your strategy, including goals, arenas, attack plans and resource deployments (Strategic Buckets) becomes a key input to developing a product roadmap. The mere specification of a strategic arena as top priority often leads to a logical list of products and projects that are necessary to enter and be successful in a chosen arena. The key question is: Given your Strategic Arenas, what major products do you need in order to win in each arena?

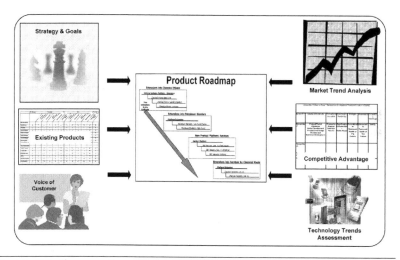

EXHIBIT 7.5: These are the many inputs to the development of a strategic product roadmap. Other inputs include the numerous sources of new product ideas, both inside and outside the firm.

Example: A major health products company identified "wound care" as a priority strategic arena (the company already sold a few products in this health care sector, but was a minor player in this market). However, once the arena "wound care" was made top priority, the specific products the firm needed to become a major force in this sector became quite evident; and, the development programs to generate these products fell into a logical sequence in a strategic product roadmap.

2. Assess Market Trends, Looking for Major New Product Opportunities

This is a forecasting exercise, and examines major market trends and shifts in your designated strategic arenas. Look back at your market analysis (Chapter 3) and ask the question: Where is this market going? And given this direction, what new products should (or could) you develop to meet these emerging market needs and trends? This market analysis includes forecasts, trend analysis, and industry analyses. It is more drill-down than the original forecast and trend analysis in Chapter 3.

In this exercise, you are often able to pinpoint specific initiatives that you must undertake in response to evident trends.

Example: The Clorox company is a producer of traditional cleaning products, dating back to the introduction of liquid bleach for laundry in 1913. Over the last decade, a new market has emerged for natural – or "green" – consumer cleaning products.[12] Clorox identified, as part of its green trend analysis, a new market segment: people looking to lessen their environmental impact on a personal and family level, in concert with the broad social "green" trend toward greater environmental consciousness.

This new segment – largely female head-of-household – was accustomed to the excellent performance of existing cleaning products, but had a desire to avoid unnecessary chemicals throughout her house. Clorox then conducted voice-of-customer research (next section) to understand what made this consumer tick. The research showed that the consumer's primary motivation was a belief that some chemicals might be dangerous to her family's health and well-being. She was primarily motivated by a safety concern rather than a generalized desire to help the environment. The target consumer, thus, became a "chemical-avoiding naturalist" who sees keeping her home and family safe as one of her main roles in life.

Working with suppliers, Clorox was able to develop a "natural" product, free of petrochemical ingredients. It is plant-derived, biodegradable, and minimally toxic to plant and animal life yet, at the same time, was an effective cleaning product that worked as well as or better than existing synthetic-based products. *Green Works* has gone on to become a great success for Clorox, exceeding the company's original expectations, and has been recognized in the top new brand ratings.

A lesson from this assessment of market trends is: Don't forget the need for peripheral vision. Clorox was quick to identify the new trend to "chemical avoidance" and, rather than ignoring the threat, turned it into an opportunity: Clorox *Green Works*. The biggest dangers are the ones you don't see coming. Understanding these threats and anticipating the opportunities requires strong peripheral vision.

3. Listen to the Voice of Your Customers

What are your customers or end-users demanding, and what is the timing? Our recent study into the best sources of new product ideas revealed voice-of-customer (VoC) research as the most effective in terms of generating breakthrough new product ideas.[13] Exhibit 7.6 shows a four quadrant diagram for ideation. It plots the relative popularity of methods (horizontal axis) and relative effectiveness (vertical axis). Note that VoC methods are all in the top, and top-right quadrants, namely the most popular and the most effective methods of ideation.

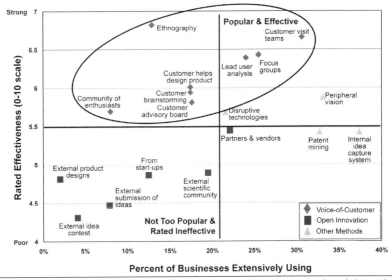

EXHIBIT 7.6: The most popular and the best methods for generating breakthrough new product ideas.[13]

Example: The pet foods division of Del Monte (US) Foods began VoC work on their "I love my dog" initiative via netnography (internet-based ethnography).[14] The company gathered and analyzed data from online blogs, forums and message boards. This enabled them to identify themes and trends in the pet food marketplace, and helped pinpoint a key segment, which they labeled "dogs are people, too".

Next, Del Monte built an online community called "I Love My Dog". This community was designed for continuous consumer interaction, and enabled a deeper consumer listening and understanding. Five hundred consumers in this segment were personally invited to participate and given password-protected access to the online community. Consumers then used the community to discuss issues, blog, chat, share photos, and find resources. They also participated in surveys from the company.

The result was a recognition of a need for a breakfast food for dogs, not unlike human food. The new product: *Snausage Breakfast Bites* was launched in 2007 and has proven a success.

Cat owners should not despair. Del Monte has also subscribed to Moms Insight Network, and has created a community of cat owners – Meow Mixer – where the company monitors discussions, tries to understand issues, gains insights, and tests concepts.

In conducting research like this, it is necessary to understand what the customer sees as value. Note that VoC is not the voice of your salesforce, nor voice of your product managers, nor is it what your scientists and engineers think. These are good sources of opinions, but are not the same as VoC research. Probe for benefits sought and customer problems or "points of pain". Focus on their unspoken, unarticulated and often hidden needs. Go beyond what customers say they want or a list of product specifications. Customer visits using interview teams, ethnography, focus groups and lead-user analysis are the top four methods for generating new product ideas in Exhibit 7.6.

4. Review Your Existing Products

In this step you take a hard look at current product offerings to decide which are tired and should be pruned and which should be replaced. Review your current product line to locate each on the product life cycle curve, as in Exhibit 7.7. Some are mature or in decline and might need enhancements, revisions or replacements.

Better yet, plot the project life cycle curves of all your products – their history as well as their forecast – as shown in Exhibit 7.8. Forecasts of your products' life cycles often reveal the need and timing for replacement products, or perhaps even a new platform if some products are tired or becoming obsolete. Additionally, gaps in the product line are identified. In this way, placemarks are inserted in your product roadmap for these required developments. The sum of these life-cycle curves may also spell trouble ahead and reveal the need for an aggressive product roadmap with many new products envisioned. Such an exercise is undertaken periodically in order to keep the product line fresh, current and complete.

Finally, review your platform evolution plan that was developed when

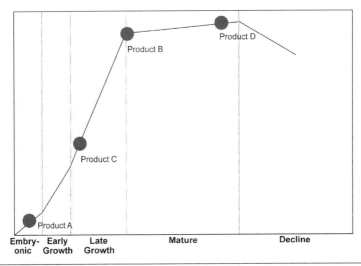

ExHIBIT 7.7: Locate your major products on the Product Life Cycle curve in order to forecast future sales and prospects. Those approaching maturity or decline are candidates for replacement or revitalization.

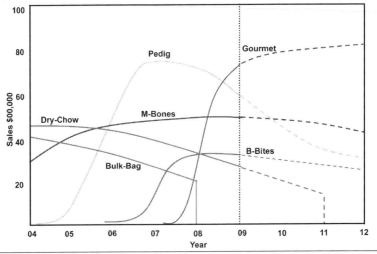

ExHIBIT 7.8: Undertake an analysis of your current products using Product Life Cycle curves (past and projected). These help you spot problems and opportunities, and the need for new initiatives in your product roadmap.

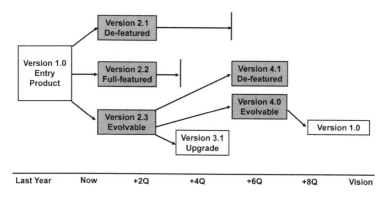

EXHIBIT 7.9: Look at your platform evolution plan, which is typically developed as part of platform strategy and business case[3]. The time might be right for some of these envisioned projects to enter your product roadmap.

the platform was originally approved.[15] Most business cases for platform developments lay out the products that will evolve or be built on that platform over time; this is called the platform evolution plan. Exhibit 7.9 shows a sample of a platform evolution plan. You will probably find that some shorter term developments are likely already in your current product roadmap, that others should be added, or that the platform evolution plan needs to be updated and revised.

5. Do a Solid Competitive Analysis

Where are your products and product lines relative to your competitors? Here, you need to assess competitors' current and probable future offerings, where they have advantage, and where your gaps are. This exercise often points to the need for new products either immediately or in the foreseeable future. Key questions include:

- How do your product offerings rate relative to competitors?
- What are your products' relative strengths or weaknesses?
- Where will your competitor's products be in one to three years?
- Which of your products need replacement or enhancement?

Example: The Australian reverse-osmosis filtration equipment company highlighted in Chapter 3 closely monitors its major competitor with similar technology located in Canada. Patent mapping or mining, trade shows, announcements in the trade press, and technical or scientific conferences are but some of the sources used in this company's competitive analysis. In this way, they anticipate what the competitor's product roadmap looks like – what new products with what capabilities they will introduce, and when – in order to be ready with products of their own.

6. Assess Technology Trends and Look for New Product Opportunities

Review your technology forecast (Chapter 3), but this time with an eye to these questions: What new products does this technology forecast make possible? Are there new products that could be built with the new or improved technology? What are they, and what are their performance characteristics?

Example: The reverse-osmosis filtration company (above) also undertakes technology forecasts regularly, mostly a prediction of expected performance the newer filter surfaces will yield (liquid throughput). The more volume that can be handled for a given surface area and pressure, the more economical, hence, competitive the filtration system becomes relative to conventional water treatment systems. This way the company is able to map out possible new products targeted at new applications that they can develop and launch, given the improvement in their filtration technology.

An equally vital question is: Given the new products that you could or would develop in the foreseeable future – your Product Roadmap – what new technologies, or new technology platforms developments will be required and what is their timing?

Example: In the cell phone industry, each new generation of cell phone includes more and more entertainment capabilities and other consumer features – taking pictures or video, watching movies online, and so on. These new features and functionality are great for cell phone users, but very demanding on technology developers. All these new features – for example, watching movies online – require much power, typically beyond the capabilities of today's batteries. So, cellphone manufacturers are diligently working on the next generation power supply technology and solution after the current lithium-ion batteries – maybe a new type of battery, maybe a fuel cell, or perhaps more energy efficient cell phones.

Another key question is: What disruptive technologies are emerging that might make differentiated new products feasible? Exhibit 7.10 shows the disruptive technology chart from Chapter 3, but this time with a difference. The figure on the left of Exhibit 7.10 shows the usual disruptive

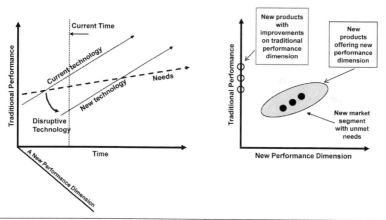

EXHIBIT 7.10:

Left diagram: The disruptive technology underperforms the current technology on the traditional performance dimension.

Right diagram: But it creates a new performance dimension. Firms that exploit the new technology thus operate on two dimensions (shaded area); those married to the old technology are stuck on the vertical dimension.

technology diagram, with the "new performance dimension" added; technology improvements are plotted against time. The figure on the right shows the two performance dimensions. The vertical axis is the traditional performance. Improvements to current products using existing technology track upwards along this vertical axis over time. The horizontal axis is new technology and its performance.

Traditional suppliers are stuck on the one vertical dimension, making product improvements over time – the small white circles. But businesses that exploit new or disruptive technology operate on the two-dimensional plane on the right side of Exhibit 7.10. Their new products are the black circles in the oval area, and deliver new functionality and performance on a totally different dimension.

It is essential that your business continually monitor the outside technology landscape in your own industry, hunting for technologies that might address current customer needs better than your own technology. Understand the dynamics of innovation and substitution, looking for an unmet customer need (or a new need) that the current technology cannot meet, and assessing whether the new technology is likely to satisfy that need. Look beyond what customers ask for; look to their real needs and benefits sought, not just their wants. And look beyond the mainstream market, identifying the handful of potential customers who stand to benefit the most from the new solution. Then seek new product opportunities!

Make a Tentative Selection of Major Initiatives

These six strategic inputs to the roadmapping exercise in Exhibit 7.5 should yield a number of new product possibilities. There are also other sources, such your own employees suggesting ideas, internal brainstorming and creativity methods, and other methods shown on the magic quadrant diagram in Exhibit 7.6[16] There are also those projects already underway and in your current roadmap, as well as "must do" products as a result of regulatory requirements or new industry standards that must be done.

At this point, the roadmapping task-force should hold an extensive, probably lengthy roadmapping session. This meeting is critical and must involve marketing managers, product managers and technology managers – an integrated and cross-functional effort. At this vital meeting, the roadmapping task-force makes a tentative selection of new, existing and proposed projects to be included in the roadmap.

The resulting Strategic Product Roadmap may look something like the map in Exhibit 7.11, which is adapted from a cell phone manufacturer.

This selection meeting is essentially a combination portfolio review and gate decision meeting:

- *Gate meeting:* Management meets to make a Go/Kill decision on a new product project (and a decision to invest resources to move to the next stage). Typically there are five gates in a Stage-Gate process for major projects, as shown in Exhibit 7.12, beginning with the idea screen, Gate 1.

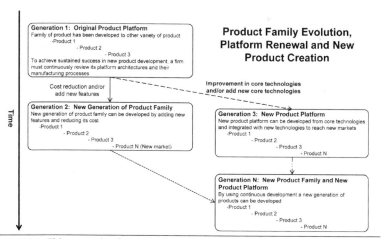

EXHIBIT 7.11: This example of a strategic product roadmap (cell phone manufacturer, disguised) reveals the evolution of products over time (verical axis) and the development of new platforms[2].

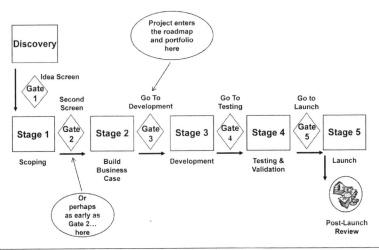

EXHIBIT 7.12: Proposed projects enter your idea-to-launch system, typically a Stage-Gate system. Projects tentatively in your product roadmap continue to be scrutinized at gates, and could be killed if warranted.

- *Portfolio review:* A portfolio review group meets to review and prioritize a set of new and on-going development projects and, in so doing, can make Go/Kill and resource commitment decisions.

Gate meetings thus tend to focus on one or a few projects, and are more in-depth on each project. Portfolio reviews look at the entire set of projects, but necessarily are a less-detailed review per project.

At this roadmapping and project selection meeting, new product projects with varying time frames must be considered. Remember that a roadmap contains projects that are proposed to be done over the next 5-7 years. Thus, new product projects under review for selection at this roadmapping meeting include:

- *Projects underway:* These are major new product projects already underway and due to be launched in the foreseeable future. These projects are already in your idea-to-launch process, in your development portfolio (if they are after Gate 2), and in your current roadmap, with a specified launch date. At the roadmapping meeting, these projects should to be confirmed for continued inclusion in an updated roadmap (or possibly removed if negative information has flowed in).

- *New but imminent projects:* These are major new projects that are proposed for an immediate start. For these proposed projects, the roadmapping meeting is equivalent to a Gate 1 idea screening meeting; projects that "pass" are inserted into the roadmap (and move into Stage 1, the Scoping stage, of the business's idea-to-launch Stage-Gate system in Exhibit 7.12).
- *Future projects:* These are proposed and major new product projects to be undertaken in the future. Placemarks are inserted in the roadmap for these future new product projects.

Use Scorecards to Make Early Go/Kill Decisions

The roadmapping task-force runs a preliminary gate/portfolio meeting for these multiple new and potential projects that are candidates for your strategic roadmap (major projects only). But how does one select the product and projects to be included in the roadmap from such a lengthy and potentially formidable list? This is no easy task, especially since most of these proposed products and projects are little more than ideas or concepts with very limited information – as one executive put it, "little more than a gleam in someone's eye".

A best practice selection method is the use of scorecards when little hard data is available for these very early-stage projects. Scorecards look at qualitative factors that are good proxies for success, profitability and strategic importance, and have proven to be a very effective method for making early Go/Kill decisions in the absence of solid financial data.[17]

A sample scorecard is shown in Exhibit 7.13, and consists of six factors, each scored by members of the roadmapping task-force or gate/portfolio review group. The total project score becomes the criterion for Go/Kill (the maximum possible score is 12 points; an average score of 60 percent or 7.2 across all evaluators is considered the minimum acceptable). The total score

CRITERIA	Low (0)	Medium (1)	High (2)	SCORE
Strategic Fit & Importance • Degree to which the idea aligns with business and/or innovation strategy	• Not aligned with business or innovation strategy	• Somewhat aligned with business and/or innovation strategy	• Aligns very well with business and/or innovation strategy	
Product & Competitive Advantage • The degree to which the idea offers unique benefits in the marketplace	• Similar to current offerings, with no or limited unique benefits	• Somewhat better than current offerings, with some unique benefits	• Significantly better than current offerings, with many unique benefits	
Market Attractiveness The degree of: • Newness of the market to the company	• Completely new and unfamiliar market	• Somewhat familiar with market	• Very familiar with market	
• Competition within the marketplace	• Strong competition within marketplace	• Modest competition within marketplace	• Weak competition within marketplace	
Synergies • Degree of fit with core competencies and strengths in marketing, manufacturing/operations, sales, and/or distribution	• No or limited fit with core competencies and strengths	• Reasonable fit with core competencies and strengths	• Strong fit with core competencies and strengths	
Technical Feasibility • Degree of familiarity of technology to the company	• Technology is completely new to company	• Technology is familiar to company	• Technology exists within company and can be leveraged	
Financial Reward vs. Risk • The size of the financial opportunity	• Poor, limited financial opportunity	• Moderate financial opportunity	• Excellent financial opportunity	
Recommendation: Go	Kill	Hold	Re-route	**SCORE TOTAL**	

EXHIBIT 7.13: Use this best-in-class scorecard for making early stage Go/Kill decisions on new product projects proposed for your product roadmap.

for each can also be used to rank and prioritize projects. Current projects already in the development pipeline (hence in the current roadmap) can also be re-scored (or use the scores from their most recent gate meeting).

Bubble Diagrams Provide An Overview of the Portfolio

Once major new product development projects have been given a tentative "yes" decision, get a feel for the nature of the resulting portfolio and roadmap. Exhibits 7.14-7.16 are useful views and employ some of the factors from the scorecard results. These portfolio bubble diagrams should include both new and existing major projects.[18]

Into Your Idea-to-Launch Gating System

By the end of this roadmapping or gate/portfolio review, your road-mapping task-force should have tentatively selected a number of new

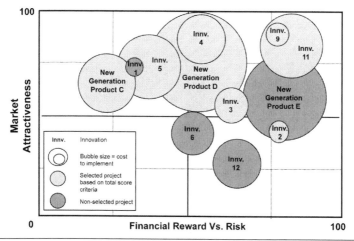

EXHIBIT 7.14: When assessing proposed projects for your product roadmap, be sure to look at the expected portfolio – both new and existing development projects. Here is one view, using two factors from the scorecard in Exhibit 7.13.

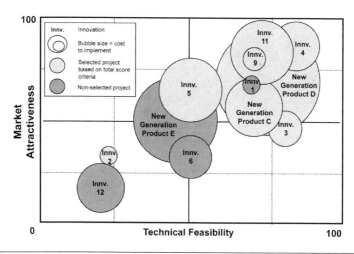

EXHIBIT 7.15: This bubble diagram reveals yet another view of the expected portfolio of development projects and is a guide to selecting the best projects for your product roadmap. Both factors are from the scorecard in Exhibit 7.13.

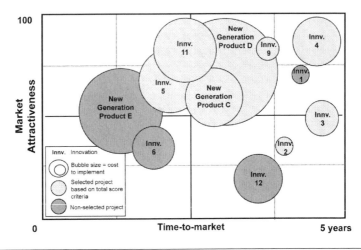

ExHIBIT 7.16: Selecting the best innovation projects for your roadmap may require multiple views. This bubble diagram uses one factor from the scorecard (Exhibit 7.13) plus time-to-market.

projects for inclusion in your roadmap (as well as confirmed those projects already underway). But note that the commitments to the new entrants are only tentative:

- Those projects that are deemed "imminent" receive limited resources and begin as early-stage projects in your gating system (they move past Gate 1 and enter Stage 1 in Exhibit 7.12).
- Some proposed projects are farther into the future, thus are simply scheduled for future development: so, a placemark on your roadmap is created. But these projects are not in your development portfolio, no financial commitments are needed for them, nor do they enter your idea-to-launch system just yet.

Once into the Stage-Gate process, a project team is formed, up-front homework and due diligence is conducted, and a business case is developed for each would-be new product. By the time the project passes Gate 3, there is strong commitment to development, and the project is "really in" the roadmap. (Note that early-stage projects – those in Stages 1 and 2 in Exhibit 7.11 – are typically ill-defined and lack key financial data, so firm commitments should not be made. These early-stage projects are only tentatively "in the roadmap".)

A Closed Loop Feedback Model

The model is a closed loop feedback system, as shown in Exhibit 7.17. The roadmapping task-force develops a tentative roadmap, and development projects enter your idea-to-launch process or Stage-Gate system. Gate meetings are held when a project completes one stage and needs resources to move to the next stage. Portfolio reviews are also held to check the health, vitality, balance and mix of development projects in the portfolio.

As projects move along, some will get into trouble – new data may suggest a negative market situation, or much more difficult and costly technical challenges – and may be de-prioritized or even killed. Other projects could begin to look better as they move forward and may be re-prioritized upwards and accelerated to market. So these ever-occurring gate meetings and portfolio reviews provide continuous feedback and changes to the portfolio of projects, which result in changes to the strategic product roadmap. It is dynamic and constantly evolving as shown in exhibit 7.17.

Example: Kennametal is a major tool component manufacturer (consumables in tooling, such as drill bits). As part of the development of their innovation strategy, one sector the business selected as high priority was the airframe industry (the company was already well-positioned in the automotive industry, especially in the US). A major VoC study of the global aircraft manufacturers – Airbus, Boeing, Bombardier, and so on – revealed that machining of landing gear was one of the most challenging machining tasks, and offered the potential for significant productivity improvements, a Kennametal forté. As a result of the VoC, a number of strategic landing gear projects were indentified and tentatively placed in the product roadmap.

Each of the projects was assigned a team leader and team to begin its way through Kennametal's ACE new product process, a very robust Stage-Gate system. But as often is the case, things don't always go according to plan. Some of the projects encountered much more serious technical hurdles than expected, and costs began to rise. For others, the market need was not as great as had originally been assumed. Thus, some of these "strategic initiatives" which looked great as they sailed through Gate 1, the idea screen, did not look nearly so profitable by the time they hit Gate 3, the Business Case approval. So management was faced with some tough choices, and (correctly) killed some of these projects, even though they were already included in the strategic roadmap.

The point is: a roadmap is evergreen, and it evolves as new information becomes available. Use the closed loop feedback concept in Exhibit 7.17 as the model, and rely on your gating system and portfolio reviews to provide the feedback and updates to the roadmapping task-force.

Make the Tough Choices!

A recurring problem is that gates in firms' new product systems are either non-existent or lack teeth.[19] The result is that, once underway, projects are rarely killed at gates, and so the needed feedback and adjustment to the roadmap in Exhibit 7.17 is missing. Rather, as one senior manager exclaimed, "Projects are like express trains, speeding down the track, slowing down at the occasional station [gate], but never stopping until they reach their ultimate destination, the marketplace".

Example: In one major high-tech communications equipment manufacturer, once a project passes Gate 1 (the idea screen), it is placed firmly into the business's product roadmap (not just tentatively). So concrete is the commitment to this early-stage project that its estimated sales and profits are now integrated into the business unit's financial forecast and plans. Once into the financial plan of the

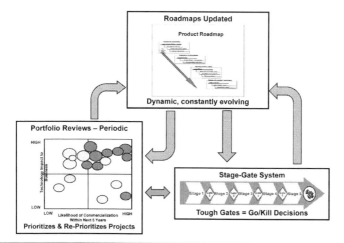

EXHIBIT 7.17: Roadmapping is part of a closed loop feedback system. New products are proposed for the roadmap. They are regularly scrutinized at both Gates and Portfolio Reviews, where they may be killed or re-prioritized.

business, the project is locked-in: there is no way that the project can be removed from the roadmap or killed. In effect, all gates after Gate 1 are merely rubber stamps.

Management in this firm simply missed the point that the idea-to-launch process is a funnel, not a tunnel; and that gates after Gate 1 are also Go/Kill points, where poor projects should be culled out. This should not be a one-gate, five-stage process. Projects in the roadmap should be scrutinized periodically at gates and portfolio reviews, and can be killed if appropriate!

Some Thoughts Before Moving Ahead

A Strategic Product Roadmap that lays out the major initiatives – developments, products and product platforms – is a powerful concept, and can be used with or without strategic buckets, which was explained in the previous chapter. Note that your roadmap should be kept to the strategic level, with placemarks for major projects, some of which are yet to be defined in detail. And it should be a timeline for the longer term, not just a list of products and projects for this year.

We have outlined an approach for developing your Strategic Product Roadmap with multiple inputs and a cross-functional roadmapping task-force of experts. The method works, and it is an excellent thought process for determining how your business will achieve its new product objectives. It also presents the elements of the plan very visually. Now, go to the next step and develop the technology roadmap, outlining what technologies are needed, and when, in order to implement the product roadmap.

Developing Your Technology Roadmap

A technology roadmap is a plan that matches short-term and long-term goals with specific technology solutions to help meet those goals. Development of a technology roadmap has three major purposes:[20] It helps reach a consensus about a set of needs and the technologies required to satisfy those needs; it provides a mechanism to help forecast technology developments; and, it provides a framework to help plan and coordinate technology developments.

Technology roadmapping is a way to develop, organize and present information about critical technology requirements and performance targets that must be met in certain timeframes. While your Strategic Product Roadmap outlines how your business will generate revenue, the technology strategy or roadmap represents all those capabilities requiring investment or alignment to achieve the key product attributes defined in your product roadmap.[21]

Technology roadmapping brings together a team of experts to develop a framework for organizing and presenting the critical technology-planning information. This enables management in your business to make the appropriate technology investment decisions, and to leverage those investments. Technology roadmapping is, thus, a needs-driven planning process designed to identify, select and develop technology alternatives to satisfy a set of product needs. It answers the basic question:

What technology must you acquire or develop — and when — in order to realize your Product Roadmap?

Developing the technology roadmap begins with definition of needs – that is, the specification of the product or products, and a delineation of the critical technology requirements and technology targets needed for those products. The next step is defining the technology areas: What technologies should be investigated that might offer a solution. For each alternative, a timeline should be estimated for how the technology will advance with respect to the technology metric or performance targets, much like the S-curve in Exhibit 4.8. These metrics are the critical variables that measure the technology performance or capabilities over time.

Your technology roadmap report is now created. Ideally your Technology Roadmap should include:[22]

- Technology development start and finish dates (may be broken down by technology readiness levels)
- Alternative technology approaches and decision points
- Start and finish dates when the technology will be commercially available
- Specific performance specs or objectives for each technology development that satisfy key product attributes in the Product Roadmap
- Technology roadmaps from critical suppliers or partners, providing technology embedded in or vital to the success of your technology development or capability.

A sample Technology Roadmap is shown in Exhibit 7.18 for a cell phone manufacturer (suitably disguised, and from a few years ago).[22] The technology areas are listed down the left side, and the technology types are shown across the map. As an example, note for "battery", nickel-cadmium was the current technology at the time this chart was drawn, to be followed by nickel-metal hydride, with up to three times the capacity. The undefined "alternate technology" turned out to be lithium-ion. And today the search is on for the next technology beyond that.

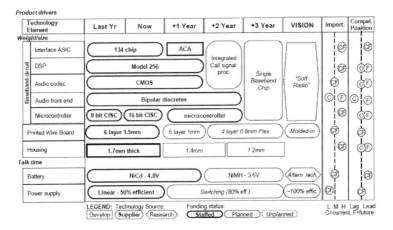

Exhibit 7.18: The Technology Roadmap underlies the Product Roadmap. The Technology Roadmap (cell phone manufacturer) is organized by critical technology area (left) and shows the critical technologies (across). Customer/market importance or priority is also shown (right).[3]

Putting Your Product Innovation Strategy to Work

We approach the end of Chapters 3 to 7 on crafting your business's innovation strategy – defining your strategic arenas, developing attack plans, strategic portfolio management, including strategic buckets and strategic roadmaps. Let's reflect on how your product innovation strategy, together with strategic portfolio management, should guide your business's development efforts.

Discovery: Searching for Product Ideas

Generating great new product ideas (labeled the "Discovery stage" in the idea-to-launch system of Exhibit 7.12) and developing a product innovation and technology strategy overlap considerably – and so they should! Indeed, progressive companies build in a heavy dose of strategy development into their Discovery stage: The search for major new product ideas begins with a strategic analysis of your marketplace (or your customer's industry) coupled with a core competencies assessment of your own business. The goal: looking for opportunities in the form of gaps, discontinuities, emerging arenas, new technologies, new platforms and unarticulated needs.

Your product innovation strategy helps to shape the Discovery stage. For example, specifying your new product arenas provides guidance to the idea search effort. Armed with a knowledge of the arenas the business wishes to target, those charged with seeking new product ideas now have a clear definition of where to search: The hunting grounds are defined. Moreover, it becomes feasible to implement formal search programs – seeking unmet customer needs and undertaking voice of customer research; initiating fundamental scientific research; implementing suggestion schemes, sales force programs and creativity sessions; and all the other methods highlighted in Exhibit 7.6 – to generate new product ideas. The search for ideas is more efficient, generating product ideas that are consistent with the business's focus.

> *Example:* Swarovski, the Austrian crystal and jewelry company, has established a best-in-class idea gathering and handling system as a front end to their Stage-Gate new product process.[23] Ideas are solicited from employees – they are easily submitted via their software system, i-Flash. Ideas go to the i-Lab – an eight-person idea support, handling and management group – where they are screened, fleshed out and defined, and made ready for presentation at Gate 1 to a business unit. But key to the success of the entire idea creation and handling system was the development of an innovation strategy for the business; just where the company wishes to focus its new product efforts. The "strategic search fields" had to be defined first, before implementing the ideation system. In three years, over 1,300 quality ideas have been generated using the i-Lab and i-Flash system.

More Effective Project Selection

The most critical criterion for selecting new product projects is whether the project is aligned with, supports and is important to your business's strategy. This is the number one scorecard question in Exhibit 7.13 and, indeed, the foremost question in virtually all project selection models. All too often, however, the question is answered with blank stares and shrugs.

A clear delineation of your business's new product arenas provides the criterion essential to answer the "strategic alignment and importance" question. Either the new product proposal under consideration fits into one of the designated arenas or it does not. And your strategic buckets guide project selection, and force limits on some types of projects. Finally, your strategic product roadmap, which defines placemarks for strategic projects, also provides directional guidance to the selection of specific development projects. The result is more effective and efficient project screening and investment decisions: Precious management time and resources are not wasted on new product proposals that may seem attractive on their own merits, but simply do not mesh with the long-term strategy or direction of the business.

Personnel and Resource Planning

Resources essential to new products – R&D, engineering, marketing, operations – cannot be acquired overnight. Without a definition of which arenas the business intends to target, and which technologies the business expects to develop or invest in, planning for the acquisition of these resources is like asking a blindfolded person to throw darts.

> *Example:* For Chempro, aerators for the pulp and paper industry is defined as one top priority arena. R&D management hired researchers in the field of biochemistry and waste treatment; the engineering department acquired new people in the field of aeration equipment design and aeration application engineering; and plans were made to add aeration experts to the salesforce. Finally, several small exploratory

technical and market research programs were initiated in aeration and bio-oxidation.

Strategic Roadmaps — Wrap-Up

Some have argued that strategic roadmapping is not much more than traditional product line planning, with more cross-functional inputs and more visual and graphic charts and outputs: "old wine in new bottles". That may be. But today's roadmapping is certainly much more complex than product line planning of days gone by. It involves many different types of people from varied functional departments – technology managers, product managers, market managers, and others – potentially working together for days at a time to agree on a set of major new product and technology initiatives envisioned over the foreseeable future. There are many and varied inputs to the discussion – strategic, market, composite and product line analysis, technology forecasts, and voice-of-customer inputs. The outputs are certainly much more visual and graphic than they used to be, which enables communicating the plan through the business more effectively.

In this chapter, we've provided you the thought process and the tools to move from strategy to tactics: a timed sequence of major product development initiatives – your Strategic Product Roadmaps. You were given many examples and illustrations to guide you as you construct your own roadmaps. Note that a roadmap is never fixed and rigid – it's a rolling and evolving one. But to paraphrase Eisenhower's earlier quotation, it's not so much the final plan or roadmap of development projects that matters; rather, the real value is the process itself – a cross-functional team of knowledgeable experts huddled together, looking at many facts, facets and factors, in order to craft your roadmap. Much like a war room with the General's staff planning a war. It's the planning process that counts, so that when things do change, or when new opportunities do arise, your organization is poised to seize the day.

CHAPTER 8

Governance – Making Your Product Innovation Strategy Work

*If management is about running the business,
governance is about seeing that it is run properly.*

R. Tricker

Governance and Your Company

Up to this point, we have devoted ourselves to the importance of strategy – of keeping an overall battle plan in sight as your product innovation strategy is created and deployed. In this chapter we explore how corporate governance structures work and the impact it has on effective implementation of your innovation strategy.

It is not enough for middle management to have an active and effective innovation framework (Stage-Gate system and portfolio prioritization); that framework must be in place from the middle on up in the organization (Strategic Arenas, Strategic Roadmapping and Strategic Buckets); and, from side-to-side (across company functions). This can be accomplished only if there is an effective and over-arching governance plan for innovation within the company.

In this chapter, some tools are provided to put formal frameworks in place to guarantee that an "innovation culture" permeates your organization, from the bottom to the top, and from the top to the bottom. We begin by clarifying our understanding of how corporate governance applies to product innovation.

The concept of governance has its roots in corporate oversight of companies and their Boards of Directors.[1] Many models have been proposed over the years, but recent years have brought increasing pressure for better governance practices. In the 1990s, institutional shareholder activism increased markedly. With the very public collapses of companies like Enron and WorldCom, and with the passage of the Sarbanes-Oxley Act in the US, there has been a further increase in corporate governance requirements. More recent difficulties within the financial industry in Europe and North America have further accentuated the need for more stringent governance and oversight.

As companies have gained experience in applying governance models, the term has become more popular and is being applied to specific aspects of the corporation. At the functional level, governance has often been applied to IT projects as managers have tried to grapple with competing demands for resources and project priorities.

Over the past few years, the term has become more widely used in product innovation – arguably one of the most complex activities an organization undertakes. Indeed, many of the lessons learned and practices used in corporate governance can be adapted to the product innovation environment. In the context of strategic product innovation, governance is about the processes through which a company implements strategy, allocates resources and makes decisions at various organizational levels, across functional areas, and among individual business areas within the company.

Does your organization's corporate governance model include product innovation?

Does Your Approach to Governance Need Improving?

If your company needs to improve its corporate governance practices with respect to product innovation, a number of easily identifiable symptoms will be evident. Generally, lack of alignment, poor cooperation across functions, and competition across groups and/or business units are early warning signals. The most tell-tale sign is a lack of clarity and transparency about the direction of your business's R&D program or total new product efforts.[2]

Other common warning flags that you may have poor governance practices are (see Exhibit 8.1 for a summary):

1. *Inefficiencies occur due to duplication of effort.* Without good co-ordination and approval, your projects and project teams from around the world are very often working on similar projects or, even worse, the same project without realizing it. Oversight of the innovation pipeline helps to ensure that different parts of your company – often with good intentions – are not duplicating each other's efforts.

2. *Decision making is not clear and is lacking in accountability.* Who is responsible for a project and how an approval is gained should not be guesswork or the result of hallway lobbying efforts. As good projects surface in your business, a clear path should exist to secure timely approvals. For this to happen, clear accountability and a clear specification of who should be making these types of decisions are needed.

3. *The right decisions are not being made.* The information to make effective investment or Go/Kill decisions is often missing or not available. A common symptom here is the uneasy feeling that your development pipeline contains too many projects that should be killed, and that it lacks the type of projects needed to meet your business goals.

4. *Resource deployment is not clearly aligned with your business's strategy.* Although your people are working hard and have a full plate of projects to work on, there is no assurance that these efforts support the strategic direction of your business. This is likely the result of weak guidelines that lack clear decision criteria.

5. *There is frustration over the value of the innovation pipeline.* Here a common symptom is the feeling that your pipeline value, if all projects were completed, would not meet desired targets. It is

probably full of time-consuming, yet low value projects. Or, worse yet, there are no realistic valuations on projects. Hence no real control and prioritization.

6. ***Business units are not following a governance process to manage innovation.*** The problem here is that each business unit spends R&D resources or consumes corporate R&D budgets, but does not utilize a proper and standard approach to selecting and funding projects; or they have no clearly defined innovation strategy. Without this type of oversight, is it very hard to have confidence in the business unit's ability to deliver results against their strategic plans.

7. ***Decisions are not timely.*** Your competitors seem to be always ahead of you and, as a result, your project teams seem to be always racing to catch up. With a poorly managed innovation strategy, organizations do not fund their strategic buckets properly. Instead, they are busy supporting short-term market requests from the sales teams. Hence, no balance exists between incremental product development projects and longer term, more strategic, major projects.

8. ***Internal politics play too large a role.*** We have all been there. More time is spent lobbying than actually doing real work. With no clear definition of roles and responsibilities, your people learn how to work the system to get things done. So a large amount of their time is spent lobbying to get or keep their budgets and people.

9. ***A lack of visibility regarding decision making.*** No one can really explain how to get approvals or how past projects were approved. Good projects lie fallow, while others seem to have a life of their own.

10. ***Frustration around the level of bureaucracy.*** Your people's frustration with the level and degree of bureaucracy is often a warning flag that existing polices and supporting documentation requirements are actually counterproductive. Stifling innovation with too much bureaucracy is very easy, particularly in a large organization. While some policies and procedures are needed, companies today are too lean to support unnecessary work.

1. Inefficiencies occur due to duplication of effort
2. Decision making is not clear and is lacking in accountability
3. Right decisions are not being made; information is lacking
4. Resource deployment is not clearly aligned with strategy
5. Frustration over the value of the innovation pipeline
6. Business units are not following a governance process to manage innovation
7. Decisions are not timely
8. Internal politics are playing too large a role
9. A lack of visibility exists into how decisions are actually made
10. Frustration around the level of bureaucracy

EXHIBIT 8.1: Ten signs your approach to governance may need to be improved.

Barriers to Adoption

Executives usually understand the need for, and desire, good governance. The problem very often lies in the fact that, internally, different groups have very different understandings of what this might mean for the company. As a result, a number of barriers to effective governance exists and must be dealt with via better communication, better processes and procedures, and a leaner decision-making approach.

Perceived red tape: Some people believe that added governance is just added bureaucracy – more management control with no tangible benefit. Indeed, in some cases this may be true where management applies too much oversight and is guilty of micromanagement. In one organization the saying was "…we spend more time and money in making the decision then the value of the funds being managed…"

Too much paperwork: The desire to develop a perfect governance model has created too much paperwork for the people charged with supplying the information. Here the common complaint is that the demands of the governance process are drowning people in completing updated reports. The process asks for too much on a too frequent basis. "Our corporation is empowered by numbers", declared one frustrated business unit executive. "I spend more time responding to head office's request for data than I do on my real job!"

Loss of flexibility and speed: The world is moving fast and your business must act in an equally rapid manner. Governance, however, can be too rigid and lack flexibility. Here the issue is seeking the mechanisms that allow change and decisions to happen in a timely fashion. Plans today are not cast in concrete and people need to be able to react quickly. The trick is to balance this need for speed with a desire for robust oversight.

Loss of control: Increased governance may be perceived as a loss of control by some people. In all businesses there are power struggles as different groups strive to maintain or increase their positions. In governance, a common concern is achieving the correct balance of power and oversight between the business unit and the needs at corporate level.

Not needed here: This declaration is heard in businesses where people pride themselves on just getting the job done and resent the fact that the organization now wants more oversight. In other companies, as they grow in size, they tend to resist the practices that larger corporations must put in place to manage a more complex company.

Who Should be Involved in Product Innovation Governance?

Strategy begins at the top and flows downward – recall Exhibit 1.4 in Chapter 1. The Product Innovation Strategy flows from (or is part of) the Business Strategy for the organization and it, in turn, drives the portfolio of projects (project selection) and the development pipeline.

The flow must also be upwards, however, as each layer builds on the information provided by work at the lower levels. This means that each decision-making layer in the company has a different governance requirement. One governance body should not manage all parts of the organization. For example, senior executive time is better spent determining and implementing innovation strategy rather than micromanaging an individual new product project.

The Innovation Pyramid (in Exhibit 8.2) provides an illustration of the various management processes that require governance. Typical governance components for each part of the Innovation Pyramid are:

- *Business Strategy:* Your business strategy defines your business's goals and objectives, and the overall strategic direction of your organization. This strategy can be at the corporate level and for each business unit (each business unit having its own goals, objectives and strategic direction, consistent with the overall corporate strategy). The Board of Directors, CEO and senior leadership team are responsible for the creation and approval of the overarching strategy of the corporation, including setting what the expectations for product innovation are to help achieve this strategic direction and goals. The leadership team of the business unit is responsible for crafting the strategy at the business unit level, including defining the role that product innovation will play in order to achieve the business's goals and objectives.

- *Product Innovation Strategy:* Your product innovation and technology strategy defines goals and identifies the Strategic Arenas for innovation. A high level version of this innovation strategy can be developed for the corporation (or for specific divisions in large divisionalized corporations with many business units within each division). Here, the CEO and the senior or corporate leadership team are responsible for developing, approving and driving the product innovation strategy that supports the business strategy. This strategy creation is often lead by the Corporate CTO (Chief Technology Officer) or Vice President of R&D. A much more specific and actionable product innovation strategy – the type we have outlined in the previous seven chapters – should also be crafted for each business unit. Those responsible usually include the leadership team of the business unit (the effort is often led by the senior technical person and/or senior marketing person).

The Innovation Pyramid **Governance**

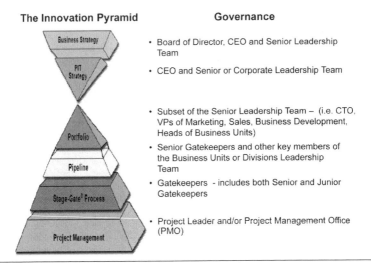

- Board of Director, CEO and Senior Leadership Team
- CEO and Senior or Corporate Leadership Team

- Subset of the Senior Leadership Team – (i.e. CTO, VPs of Marketing, Sales, Business Development, Heads of Business Units)
- Senior Gatekeepers and other key members of the Business Units or Divisions Leadership Team
- Gatekeepers - includes both Senior and Junior Gatekeepers
- Project Leader and/or Project Management Office (PMO)

EXHIBIT 8.2: Each aspect of the Innovation Pyramid has a governance requirement.

- *Portfolio Management:* Portfolio management operationalizes the product innovation and technology strategy by making the strategic investment decisions for product innovation (for example, deciding Strategic Buckets or developing the Strategic Product Roadmap). For most corporations, portfolio management occurs at the business unit level (although some corporations also elevate portfolio management to the divisional level or even to the corporate level). At the business unit, those responsible for portfolio management include a portfolio team comprised of a subset of the leadership team of the business, for example the heads of technology, marketing, sales, business development and often the head of the business unit itself. This group ensures that the strategic direction of the portfolio supports the business's product innovation strategy and that the spending allocations, or spending in arenas, is in line with the strategic intent and direction of that strategy. When done at the corporate (or divisional) level, those responsible for portfolio management usually include the Corporate CTO or Vice President of R&D, the CMO (Chief Marketing Officer), the head of business development, and the heads of the business units.

- *Pipeline Portfolio:* Pipeline portfolio management (referred to earlier as tactical portfolio management in Exhibit 6.4) prioritizes individual development projects and tactically allocates resources – people and money – to these projects. Members of the business unit's leadership team are responsible for overseeing the pipeline of projects. This portfolio review team meets periodically to review the entire portfolio of projects at portfolio review meetings, looking at project prioritization, the mix and balance of projects, and the appropriateness of resource allocations, ensuring that resources are in place to achieve a timely completion of projects.

- *Stage-Gate Process:* The Stage-Gate process guides and directs the efforts on individual development projects from idea through to launch, including making approval (Go/Kill) decisions and resource commitment decisions on specific projects. The governance groups are called the "Gatekeepers"; the Gatekeepers at each gate are the owners of the resources required to progress the project through the next stage.

    Usually the senior Gatekeepers make the decisions on major projects at the major investment gates, namely Gates 3, 4 and 5 in Exhibit 7.12; they are usually the leadership team of the business. Managers at the next level down are often the Gatekeepers at the earlier gates (Gates 1 and 2 in Exhibit 7.12 where investments are smaller) or at all the gates for less risky or smaller, lower cost projects.

- *Project Management:* Project management oversees the budgets and milestones of individual projects. Development projects are led by designated project leaders, who often assume the dual role of both project leader and project manager. Normally the project leader is viewed as the entrepreneurial head of the project, leading his or her project team, developing objectives, proposals and plans for the project, seeking management's support, and so on – much like the leader in a small business start-up. By contrast, the project manager is more a "nuts and bolts" administrative manager, responsible for timelines, budgets, scheduling team meetings, documentation, etc. In some firms, and for larger development projects, there is both a team leader and a project manager, the latter often is assigned from the PMO (project management office).

The What, Why, Who of Governance

Typically, a governance model is developed to ensure that the various aspects of product innovation receive the proper and appropriate levels of oversight to ensure that the strategy and goals of the organization will be achieved. The first step is to identify what your Innovation Pyramid should look like. Most companies adopt a model very similar to the Innovation Pyramid just described and illustrated in Exhibit 8.2.

Once the different levels in your pyramid framework have been decided, the next step is to agree upon a set of decisions that each of these levels is, in turn, responsible for. At the Stage-Gate level, for example, Gatekeepers have the responsibility for approving projects and committing appropriate resources to move them forward to the next stage in the development process.

Roles and responsibilities must be defined and agreed upon. Each participant in each layer of governance must understand their roles and responsibilities, as well as the boundaries of their particular governance role. Each layer of governance must also be able to interact with the groups above and below to ensure there is good continuity and no overlap of authority or duplication in effort. Clear direction and definition of what is being governed at each step is important for organizational clarity.

Typically, to ensure timely and effective oversight, most governance groups agree on a timeframe or meeting schedule to ensure timely fulfillment of responsibilities. For example, the group responsible for strategic portfolio management might have a regularly scheduled meeting, perhaps

EXHIBIT 8.3: Components of a high-level governance model.

of resources, make any changes needed, and make recommendations for spending and approvals for the upcoming quarter.

Some companies also make an effort to define behavior expectations for each group. In practice, at the more senior level, seeking the right behaviors by management at these governance meetings is often a challenge. For example, the leadership team of the business already has a working style and culture that is effective in running the rest of the business, and probably is not all that receptive to a new set of rules for themselves just for innovation governance. Instead, it is better to try and leverage existing protocols and focus on making sure they understand what the purpose of the role is and how it will impact the company. However, as one moves lower in the organization, very often clear rules of engagement and clear expectations of behavior are more common. For example, project leadership and project oversight have very clearly defined roles and responsibilities and even good descriptions of what an effective project leader is. Also, many companies have very clear "rules of engagement" for gatekeepers to ensure that these meetings run effectively.[3]

The final aspect in implementation of your innovation governance is oversight; ensuring that the governance process functions well in your organization. Here it is important to have a senior executive who has clear accountability for making the governance process work. If no one is in charge of the process, then do not be surprised if it is very haphazard and ineffective in your company.

Example: Corning, a five billion dollar sales company and a world leader in specialty glass and ceramics, has a long track record of successful product innovation. To facilitate the need for continuous innovation, the corporate innovation pipeline is governed by two key innovation councils (Exhibit 8.4).[4]

1. The Corporate Technology Council for the early stage opportunities and research programs

2. The Growth and Strategy Council for later stage programs growing to become product lines or new businesses.

The councils are chaired by leaders in the company, who meet once a month to review programs and assess the corporate innovation priorities. The heads of RD&E and New Business Development sit on both councils to provide continuity.

The third governance body is the Board of Directors. Beginning about five years ago, regular briefing sessions were held to update the Board. At first these sessions were voluntary, but they proved so compelling that the "Technology with the Board" sessions are now attended by all Board members, and is now part of the Board meeting structure.

Corning also uses what they call a "Corporate Innovation Process Group" that oversees the deployment and application of Stage-Gate and the other innovation processes across the corporation. Their mandate is to drive continuous process improvement. Each Division manages its own pipeline of projects.

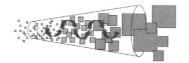

Corporate Innovation Portfolio

Corporate Technology Council	Growth & Strategy Council
Long term growth	Medium term growth
Stage I – II	Stage II - IV
Identify, assess, develop	Sort, pace, execute
Technology/opportunity focus	Commercialization focus
CTO + RD&E & NBD Leaders	CEO, COO, CTO + CTO Staff

**Technology & Strategy updates presented to the
Board of Directors**

EXHIBIT 8.4: Corning uses two types of innovation pipeline governance groups to manage long term and medium term growth.[4]

In designing and implementing your governance model and the approach to use, keep in mind some common best practice themes. First, each company's needs are different; hence, like most business models, one approach does not fit all companies. You must tailor your own innovation governance model to match your company's needs and culture, and to fit the size of your organization. Second, your governance model should reflect your company's organizational structure and design, particularly its global structure; it should also provide a good balance between the needs of the business units (for autonomy and control) and the needs of the corporate head office (for control and information). Next, all the key decision-makers must be a part of the governance model. This includes the corporate leadership team, as well as leadership teams from all regions, business units and key functional areas. Next, the governance model must be visible: A model is only good if it engages people and is widely known and understood. Finally, in today's rapidly changing business environment, your governance model must be flexible and adaptable, adjusting to your ever-changing company environment, both external and internal.

Wrap-Up

This brings to an end our guide to formulating a product innovation strategy… or maybe it's just the beginning for you and your business. You've seen the evidence – how important a product innovation strategy is, and what a strong positive impact such a strategy has on performance. In Chapters Two to Seven we've laid out a pathway for developing this strategy for your business. In this chapter, we have shown how governance in your organization plays a vital role in ensuring that all these components of your strategy work together.

Follow the flow and thought process in Exhibit 3.3. The pathway begins with your goals and objectives (Chapter 2) and moves on to resource deployment decisions, namely, Strategic Buckets and Strategic Roadmaps (Chapters 6 and 7). It ends with putting in place a governance structure that fosters successful innovation in your company.

If you're thinking that your business lacks a clearly articulated innovation strategy and that maybe now is the time to lay the groundwork for developing one, you're probably right on both counts. The first step on a major journey is the longest one. The first action item is getting support from others in your organization – to really "sell" your colleagues on the need for an innovation strategy and that there is, indeed, a proven way to develop an effective strategy. Letting them read this book will be a start. The second step is to put together a task-force charged with crafting an innovation strategy. The third step is…. well, you get the point… so keep moving forward.

ENDNOTES

Chapter 1

1. This case study is based on research: Abel, I., "From technology imitation to market dominance: The case of the iPod", *Competitiveness Review, An International Business Journal,* 18:3, 2008, pp. 257-274.

2. Frommer, D., "Apple Q1: The iPod has left the building", *Business Insider: Silicon Alley Insider,* January 22, 2008.

3. Stross, R., "How iPod ran circles around the Walkman," *The New York Times,* 2005, available at *http://nytimes.com/2005/03/13/business/worldbusiness/13digi.html.*

4. The authors conducted a major benchmarking study of new product performance and practices with the APQC (American Productivity and Quality Center, Houston, TX), hereafter called "The Benchmarking Study"; see: *Best Practices in Product Development: What Distinguishes Top Performers,* at *www.prod-dev.com;* also: Cooper, R.G., Edgett, S.J., & Kleinschmidt, E.J., "Benchmarking best NPD practices – Part 1: Culture, climate, teams and senior management's role", *Research-Technology Management,* 47:1, January-February 2004, pp. 31-43; also: Cooper, R. G., Edgett, S.J. & Kleinschmidt, E.J., "Benchmarking best NPD practices – Part 2: Strategy, resources and portfolio management practices", *Research-Technology Management,* 47:3, May-June 2004, pp. 50-60; and: Cooper, R.G., Edgett, S.J. & Kleinschmidt, E. J., "Benchmarking best NPD practices – Part 3: The NPD process & decisive idea-to-launch activities", *Research-Technology Management,* 47:6, January-February 2005, pp. 43-55. See also: Cooper, R.G. and Edgett, S.J., "Maximizing productivity in product innovation", *Research Technology Management,* 51:2, March-April 2008, pp. 47-58.

5. Parts of this chapter appeared in: Cooper, R.G., *Product Leadership: Pathways to Profitable Innovation,* 2nd edition. New York, NY: Perseus Publishing, 2005. See also: Cooper, R.G., "Product innovation & technology strategy", reprinted in *Succeeding in Technological Innovation,* Washington: Industrial Research Institute, May 2001, pp. 14-17; and parts are also taken from: Cooper, R.G., *Winning at New Products: Accelerating the Process from Idea to Launch,* 3rd edition. Reading, MA: Perseus Books, 2001.

6. APQC benchmarking study, see endnote 4.

7. The Innovation Diamond is explained in more detail in: Cooper, R.G., *Winning at New Products: Pathways to Profitable Innovation*, Microsoft whitepaper, 2005. Or online at *www.stage-gate.com*.

8. A comprehensive view of portfolio management methods is in: Cooper, R.G., Edgett, S.J., & Kleinschmidt, E.J., *Portfolio Management for New Products, 2nd edition.* New York, NY: Perseus Publishing, 2002. Also: Cooper, R.G. and Edgett, S.J., "Ten ways to make better portfolio and project selection decisions", PDMA *Visions Magazine*, XXX:3, June 2006, pp. 11-15.

9. *Stage-Gate®* is a registered trademark of the Product Development Institute Inc., and is a term originally coined by Robert Cooper, one of the authors. See: Cooper, R.G., *Winning at New Products: Accelerating the Process from Idea to Launch*, 3rd edition. Reading, MA: Perseus Books, 2001.

10. Cooper, R.G., "How companies are re-inventing their idea-to-launch methodologies", *Research-Technology Management*, 52:2, March-April 2009, pp. 47-57.

11. Cooper, R.G. & Mills, M., "Succeeding at new products the P&G way: A key element is using the Innovation Diamond", *PDMA Visions*, XXIX:4, October 2005, pp. 9-13.

12. The P&G Initiatives Diamond is taken from Cooper & Mills, see endnote 11.

13. Lafley. A.G. & Charan, R., *The Game-Changer*, Crown Publishing Group, Random, House, New York, NY, 2008.

14. APQC study, see endnote 4.

15. Source: US Army FM-3-0 of Military Operations (sections 4-32 to 4-39).

16. Luck, D.J. & Prell, A.E., *Market Strategy*. Englewood Cliffs, N.J.: Prentice Hall, 1968, p. 2.

17. Ansoff, I.H., *Corporate Strategy*, New York, NY: McGraw-Hill, 1965.

18. Corey, R.E. "Key options in market selection and product planning," *Harvard Business Review*, September-October 1978, pp. 119-128.

19. Some sections in this chapter are taken from a book by the authors: Cooper, R.G., Edgett, S.J. & Kleinschmidt, E.J., *Portfolio Management for New Products, 2nd edition.* Reading, Mass: Perseus Books, 2002.

20. Crawford, C.M., "Protocol: New tool for product innovation", *Journal of Product Innovation Management*, 2, 1984, pp. 85-91.

21. Menke, M.M., "Essentials of R&D strategic excellence," *Research-Technology Management*, 40:5, September-October 1997, pp. 42-47.

22. Booz-Allen & Hamilton. *New Product Management for the 1980s.* New York: Booz-Allen & Hamilton Inc., 1982.

23. See endnote 4.

24. The Cooper strategy studies: Cooper, R.G., "Industrial firms' new product strategies," *Journal of Business Research*, 13, April 1985, pp. 107-121; and: Cooper, R.G., "Overall corporate strategies for new product programs", *Industrial Marketing Management*, 14, 1985, pp. 179-183.

25. Strategic buckets is explained in the portfolio management sources in endnote 8.

26. See: Albright, R.E. & Kappel, T.A., "Roadmapping in the corporation", *Research-*

Technology Management, 46:2, March-April, 2003, pp. 31-40; also: McMillan, A., "Roadmapping – agent of change", *Research-Technology Management,* 46:2, March-April, 2003, pp. 40-47; and: Myer, M.H. and Lehnerd, A.P., *The Power of Product Platforms.* New York, NY: Free Press, 1997.

27. Parts of this section are taken from an article by the author: Cooper, R.G., "Maximizing the value of your new product portfolio: Methods, metrics and scorecards", *Current Issues in Technology Management,* published by Stevens Alliance for Technology Management, 7:1, Winter 2003, p. 1.

Chapter 2

1. Mills, M., "Implementing a Stage-Gate process at Procter & Gamble," *Proceedings, First International Stage-Gate® Conference,* St. Petersburg Beach, FL, February 2007.

2. Cooper, R.G. & Mills, M., "Succeeding at new products the P&G way: A key element is using the Innovation Diamond", *PDMA Visions,* XXIX:4, October 2005, pp. 9-13.

3. See benchmarking study, endnote 4 in Chapter 1.

4. Booz-Allen & Hamilton: see endnote 22 in Chapter 1.

5. Booz-Allen & Hamilton: see endnote 22 in Chapter 1.

6. See benchmarking study, endnote 4 in Chapter 1.

7. Maxwell, C., "A disciplined approach to innovation", *Proceedings, Second International Stage-Gate® Conference,* Clearwater Beach, FL, February 2008.

8. Erler, J., "A brilliant new product idea generation program: Swarovski's i-Lab story", *Proceedings, Second International Stage-Gate® Conference,* Clearwater Beach, FL, February 2008.

9. Source of attrition curve data: PDMA (Product Development & Management Association) studies: Adams, M. & Boike, D., "PDMA foundation CPAS study reveals new trends", *Visions,* XXVIII:3, July 2004, pp. 26-29; and: Adams, M. *The PDMA Foundation's 2004 Comparative Performance Assessment Study (CPAS). www.pdma.org*

10. Griffin, A. & Page, A.L., "PDMA success measurement project: Recommended measures for product development success and failure", *Journal of Product Innovation Management,* 13:6, November 1996, pp. 478-495.

11. Arra, R., "Value Based Product Development (VBPD): ITT's initiative to improve product generation", *Proceedings, Third International Stage-Gate Conference,* Clearwater Beach, FL, February 2009.

12. Source: Albright, R.E., "Roadmaps and roadmapping: Linking business strategy and technology planning," *Proceedings, Portfolio Management for New Product Development,* Institute for International Research and Product Development & Management Association, Ft. Lauderdale, FL, January 2001.

Chapter 3

1. Strategy studies: see Chapter 1, endnote 21.
2. Day, G.S., "A strategic perspective on product planning," *Journal of Contemporary Business,* Spring 1975, pp. 1-34.
3. Based on maps in: Gadiesh, O. & Gilbert, J.L., "How to map your industry's profit pool", *Harvard Business Review,* May-June 1998, pp. 3-11.
4. Porter, M.E., *Competitive Advantage: Creating and Sustaining Superior Performance.* New York, NY: Free Press, 1985.
5. For an excellent description of the principles and method of peripheral vision, see: Day, G.S. & Shoemaker, P., "Scanning the periphery", *Harvard Business Review,* November 2005, p 135-148. Parts of this section on peripheral vision are based on this article.
6. Fuld-Gilad-Herring Academy of Competitive Intelligence.
7. See: Christensen, C.M., *The Innovator's Dilemma,* New York, NY: Harper Collins, 2000.
8. Foster, R.N. *Innovation: The Attacker's Advantage.* Summit Books, 1988.
9. See success drivers in: Montoya-Weiss, M.M. & Calantone, R.J., "Determinants of new product performance: A review and meta analysis", *Journal of Product Innovation Management,* 11:5, November. 1994, pp. 397-417; and: Cooper, R. G., Chapter 1 "New products: What separates the winners from the losers" in: *The PDMA Handbook of New Product Development, 2nd Edition,* New York, NY: John Wiley & Sons, 2004.
10. Hamel, G. & Prahalad, C.K. *Competing for the Future:* Cambridge, MA: Harvard Business School Press, April 1996.

Chapter 4

1. Day, G.S., "A strategic perspective on product planning," *Journal of Contemporary Business,* Spring 1975, pp. 1-34.
2. Source of the Corning case: Kirk, B., "Creating an environment for effective innovation." *Proceedings, Third International Stage-Gate Conference,* Clearwater Beach, FL, February 2009.
3. Corey, R.E., "Key options in market selection and product planning", *Harvard Business Review,* September.-October. 1978, pp. 119-128.
4. Abell, D.F., *Defining the Business.* Englewood Cliffs, N.J.: Prentice Hall, 1980.
5. Crawford, C.M., "Protocol: new tool for product innovation", *Journal of Product Innovation Management,* 2, 1984, pp. 85-91.
6. Based on: Cooper, R.G., "Defining the new product strategy", *IEEE Trans. on Engineering Management,* EM-34:6. 1987, pp. 184-193; Cooper, R.G., "Identifying and evaluating new product opportunities" in: Day, G.S., Weitz, B. & Wensley, R.,

The Interface of Marketing and Strategy, Vol. 4 of the series: *Strategic Management Policy and Planning: A Multivolume Treatise.* Greenwich, CT: JAI Press Inc, 1990. See also: Cooper, R.G., "Product innovation and technology strategy", reprinted in *Succeeding in Technological Innovation,* Washington: Industrial Research Institute, May 2001, pp. 14-17.

Chapter 5

1. Miles, R.E. & Snow, C.C., *Organizational Strategy, Structure and Process.* New York: McGraw-Hill, 1978.
2. These definitions are taken from an article by Griffin and Page, who provide a breakdown of project types by strategy elected; see: Griffin, A. and Page, A.L., "PDMA success measurement project: Recommended measures for product development success and failure", *Journal of Product Innovation Management,* 13:6, November 1996, pp. 478-495.
3. See PDMA CPAS study, endnote 9 in Chapter 2.
4. Source of Corning example: Kirk, B., "Creating an environment for effective innovation." *Proceedings, Third International Stage-Gate Conference,* Clearwater Beach, FL, February 2009.
5. These strategy types are based on concepts from several sources: Porter, M.E., *Competitive Advantage: Creating and Sustaining Superior Performance.* New York: Free Press, 1985; also: the Cooper strategy studies, Chapter 1, endnote 24.
6. Source: Bijapurkar, R., "10 Biz Ideas That Changed India", *The Week,* Aug 31, 2008, p 17.
7. Paragraph taken from: Cooper, R., "The state of product development: Letter from India", *Research-Technology Management,* 52:1, 2009, pp. 6-7.
8. Kleinschmidt, E.J. & Cooper, R.G., "The performance impact on an international orientation of product innovation," *European Journal of Marketing,* 22, 1988, pp. 56-71; also: Cooper, R.G. & Kleinschmidt, E.J., *New Products: The Key Factors in Success.* Chicago: American Marketing Assoc., 1990.
9. Roberts, E.B. & Berry, C.A., "Entering new businesses: Selecting strategies for success", *Sloan Management Review,* Spring 1983, pp. 3-17.
10. Roberts, E.B., "New ventures for corporate growth", *Harvard Business Review,* 1980, pp. 3-17.
11. Roberts, E.B. & Berry, C.A.: See endnote 9.
12. See success factors in: Montoya-Weiss, M.M. & Calantone, R.J., "Determinants of new product performance: A review and meta analysis", *Journal of Product Innovation Management,* 11:5, November 1994, pp. 397-417; and: Cooper, R. G., Chapter 1 "New products: What separates the winners from the losers" in: *The PDMA Handbook of New Product Development, 2nd Edition,* New York, NY: John Wiley & Sons, 2004.

13. Killing, J.P., "Diversification through licensing," *R&D Management,* 1978, pp. 159-163.

14. Roberts, E.B.: see endnote 10.

15. Killing, J.P.: see endnote 13.

16. Roberts, E.B.: see endnote 10.

17. Roberts, E.B.: see endnote 10.

18. Lafley, A.G. & Charan, R., *The Game-Changer.* Crown Publishing Corporate. Division of Random House, New York, 2008.

19. Parts of this section are adapted from: Chesbrough, H., "'Open innovation' myths, realities, and opportunities", *Visions,* April 2006.

20. Examples adapted from: Chesbrough, H., endnote 19.

21. Source; Chesbrough, H., *Open Innovation: The New Imperative for Creating and Profiting from Technology,* Harvard Business School Press, 2003.

22. Parts of this section are adapted from: Docherty, M., "Primer on 'open innovation': Principles and practice", *Visions,* April 2006.

23. Source: Chesbrough, H., *Visions,* endnote 19.

24. Adapted from Docherty, M., *Visions,* endnote 22.

25. Example adapted from: *Open Innovation,* QuickMBA.

26. The section relies on material from P&G's "Connect + Develop" webpage, as well as from internal private communications. See: *www.pgconnectdevelop.com.* See also: Huston, L. and Sakkab, N., "Connect + Develop: Inside Procter & Gamble's new model for innovation," *Harvard Business Review,* 84:3, March 2006.

27. Tao, J. & Magnotta, V., "How Air Products and Chemicals 'identifies and accelerates'", *Research-Technology Management,* September-October 2006, pp 12-18.

28. Some examples in this section are adapted from: Docherty, M., *Visions,* endnote 22.

29. "An Idea with Bounce", *Technology Review,* April 2005.

30. Parts of this section on the benefits of open innovation are adapted from Docherty, M., *Visions,* endnote 22.

31. *Collaborating to Grow,* KPMG Study, cited in *Industry Week* article, August. 1, 2005.

32. Source of GE quotes: "The move toward open innovation is beginning to transform entire industries", *The Economist* print edition, October 11, 2007.

33. Gann, D. and Dahlander, L., as quoted in the *Economist;* see endnote 32.

Chapter 6

1. This chapter is based on a number of books and articles by the authors and co-worker: Cooper, R.G., *Product Leadership: Pathways to Profitable Innovation,* 2nd edition. New York, NY: Perseus Publishing, 2005. Cooper, R.G., Edgett, S.J. & Kleinschmidt, E.J., *Portfolio Management for New Products, 2nd edition.* Reading, Mass: Perseus Books, 2002; Cooper, R.G., *Winning at New Products: Accelerating the Process from Idea to Launch, 3rd edition.* Reading, MA: Perseus Books, 2001; a three part series by Cooper,

R.G., Edgett, S.J. & Kleinschmidt, E.J., "Portfolio management in new product development: Lessons from the leaders – Part I", *Research-Technology Management*, September-October 1997, pp. 16-28; Part II, November-December 1997, pp. 43-57; Cooper, R.G., Edgett, S. J. & Kleinschmidt, E.J., "New problems, new solutions: Making portfolio management more effective", *Research-Technology Management*, 2000, 43:2, pp. 18-33; and: Cooper, R.G., Edgett, S.J. & Kleinschmidt, E.J., "Portfolio management: Fundamental to new product success", in The *PDMA Toolbox for New Product Development*, edited by Beliveau, P., Griffin, A. & Somermeyer, S. New York, NY: John Wiley & Sons, Inc., 2002, pp. 331-364.

2. APQC benchmarking study: see endnote 4 in Chapter 1. Available as: *Best Practices in Product Development: What Distinguishes Top Performers*, at *www.prod-dev.com*.

3. Parts of this section are taken from an article by the authors: Cooper, R.G. & Edgett, S.J., "Overcoming the crunch in resources for new product development", *Research-Technology Management*, 46:3, 2003, pp. 48-58.

4. APQC benchmarking study: see endnote 2.

5. The conclusions regarding new product resource problems and causes are based on several benchmarking studies cited previously: see endnotes 4 and 5 in Chapter 1. Also two portfolio management studies; see endnote 1 and: Cooper, R.G., Edgett, S.J. & Kleinschmidt, E.J., "Portfolio management for new product development: Results of an industry practices study," *R&D Management*, 31:4, October. 2001, pp. 361-380.

6. APQC benchmarking study: see endnote 2.

7. APQC benchmarking study: see endnote 2.

8. Earlier benchmarking studies by Cooper and Kleinschmidt: see: Cooper, R.G., "Benchmarking new product performance: Results of the best practices study", *European Management Journal*, 16:1, 1998, pp. 1-7; Cooper, R.G. & Kleinschmidt, E.J., "Winning businesses in product development: Critical success factors", *Research-Technology Management*, 39;4, July-August 1996, pp. 18-29; Cooper, R.G. & Kleinschmidt, E.J., "Benchmarking the firm's critical success factors in new product development", *Journal of Product Innovation Management*, 12:5, November 1995, pp. 374-391; also: Cooper, R.G. & Kleinschmidt, E.J., "Benchmarking firms' new product performance and practices", *Engineering Management Review*, 23:3, Fall 1995, pp. 112-120; and Cooper, R.G. & Kleinschmidt, E.J., "Winning businesses in product development: Critical success factors", *Research-Technology Management*, 39:4, July-August 1996, pp. 18-29.

9. See: Cooper & Edgett, endnote 3.

10. Source: Cooper, R.G. *Winning at New Products: Accelerating the Process from Idea to Launch, 3rd edition*. Reading, MA: Perseus Books, 2001. Chapter 2 provides a good overview of quality of execution in new product projects, and insights into which activities are particularly weak.

11. Success/failure studies; see success drivers in: Montoya-Weiss, M.M. & Calantone, R.J., "Determinants of new product performance: A review and meta analysis", *Journal of Product Innovation Management*, 11:5, November. 1994, pp. 397-417; and: Cooper,

R. G., Chapter 1 "New products: What separates the winners from the losers" in: *The PDMA Handbook of New Product Development, 2nd Edition,* New York, NY: John Wiley & Sons, 2004; also the *NewProd®* studies: see endnote [10], Chapters 2-4.

12. Source: see Cooper & Edgett, endnote 3.

13. The results of the study into portfolio management practices in industry are in: Cooper, R.G., Edgett, S.J. & Kleinschmidt E.J., "Portfolio management in new product development: Lessons from the leaders – Part I", *Research-Technology Management,* 40:5, September-October 1997, pp. 16-28; and: Cooper, R.G., Edgett, S.J., & Kleinschmidt E.J., "Portfolio management in new product development: Lessons from the leaders – Part II", *Research-Technology Management,* 40;6, November-December 1997, pp. 43-52; also: Cooper, R.G., Edgett, S.J. & Kleinschmidt E.J., "Best practices for managing R&D portfolios", *Research-Technology Management,* 41;4, July-August 1998, pp. 20-33.

14. A second major benchmarking study into portfolio management practices probes portfolio management practices and performance; undertaken with the Industrial Research Institute. Results are in: Cooper, R.G., Edgett, S.J. & Kleinschmidt, E.J., "New product portfolio management: practices and performance", *Journal of Product Innovation Management,* 16:4, July 1999, pp. 333-351; and: Cooper, R.G., Edgett, S.J. & Kleinschmidt, E.J., "Portfolio management for new product development: Results of an industry practices study", *R&D Management,* 31:4, October 2001, pp. 361-380.

15. Crawford, C.M., "The hidden costs of accelerated product development", *Journal of Product Innovation Management,* 9:3, September 1992, pp. 188-199.

16. See: Cooper & Edgett, endnote 3.

17. The BCG model is described and assessed in: Heldey, B., "Strategy and the business portfolio", *Long Range Planning,* 1977; and: Day, G., *Analysis for Strategic Marketing Decisions,* St. Paul, MN: West Publishing, 1986.

18. Griffin, A. & Page, A., "PDMA success measurement project: Recommended measures for product development success and failure", *Journal of Product Innovation Management,* 13:6, November 1996, pp. 478-496.

19. APQC benchmarking study: see endnote 2.

20. Earlier benchmarking studies by Cooper & Kleinschmidt: see endnote 8.

21. Parts of this section and the box insert describing "Your business's new product objectives – resource demand-versus-capacity analysis" is modified from: Cooper, R.G., "The invisible success factors in product innovation", *Journal of Product Innovation Management,* 16:2, April 1999, pp. 115-133.

22. Industrial Research Institute's 10th Annual R&D Leaderboard, Research & Technology Management, 51:6, November-December 2008, page 15.

23. *Science & Engineering Indicators,* Chapter 4, "Research and development: National trends and international linkages", National Science Foundation, 2008. *www.nsf.gov/statistics/seind08/c4/c4s3.htm*

24. As reported in: Cooper, R.G. *Winning at New Products: Accelerating the Process from Idea to Launch, 3rd edition.* Reading, MA: Perseus Books, 2001, Chapter 2.

25. For more detail on "resource demand-versus-capacity analysis", see: Cooper, endnote 21.

26. For practical approaches on how to effectively prune the portfolio, see: Cooper, R.G., "Effective gating: Make product innovation more productive by using gates with teeth", *Marketing Management Magazine*, March-April 2009, pp 12-17.

27. Source: Booz-Allen & Hamilton, *Global Innovation Survey*, New York, NY: Oct 2005.

28. Cooper, R.G. & Kleinschmidt, E.J., "Winning businesses in product development: The critical success factors", updated, *Research-Technology Management*, 50:3, May-June 2007, pp 52-66.

29. This section taken from: Booz-Allen & Hamilton report, endnote 27.

30. Portfolio management is defined in: Cooper, R.G., Edgett, S.J. & Kleinschmidt, E.J., "Portfolio management in new product development: Lessons from the leaders – Part I", *Research-Technology Management*, September-October 1997, pp. 16-28; Part II, November-December 1997, pp. 43-57.

31. Parts of this section are taken from an article by one of the authors: Cooper, R.G., "Maximizing the value of your new product portfolio: Methods, metrics and scorecards", *Current Issues in Technology Management*. Hoboken, N.J.: Stevens Institute of Technology, Stevens Alliance for Technology Management, 7:1, Winter 2003, p. 1.

32. Excellent methods for tactical portfolio management, namely project selection, are in: Cooper, R.G. & Edgett, S.J., "Ten ways to make better portfolio and project selection decisions", PDMA *Visions Magazine*, XXX:3, June 2006, pp. 11-15; also: Cooper, R.G., Edgett, S.J. and Kleinschmidt, E.J., *Portfolio Management for New Products, 2nd edition*. Reading, MA: Perseus Books, 2002.

33. The results in this section are from the APQC benchmarking study: see endnote 2. Many of the examples cited are from this study as well.

34. Bull, S., "Innovating for Success: How EXFO's NPDS Delivers Winning Products", Proceedings, First International Stage-Gate Conference, St. Petersburg Beach, FL, February 2007.

35. Source: MARS Petfoods Australia, Catriona Giffard, R&D Manager. Numbers are disguised. Used with permission.

36. The split in EXFO's portfolio is found in endnote 34.

37. Roberts, E. & Berry, C., "Entering new businesses: Selecting strategies for success", *Sloan Management Review*, Spring, 1983, pp. 3-17.

38. See project selection and ranking methods in endnote 31.

Chapter 7

1. Whalen, P.J., "Strategic and technology planning on a roadmapping foundation", *Research-Technology Management*, 50:3, May-June 2007, pp 40-51.

2. This section on roadmapping draws on many sources, including Alcatel-Lucent Technologies (Bell Labs). See: Albright, R.E., "Roadmaps and roadmapping: Linking

business strategy and technology planning", *Proceedings, Portfolio Management for New Product Development*, Institute for International Research and Product Development & Management Association, Ft. Lauderdale, FL, January 2001. See also: Meyer, M.H. & Lehnerd, A.P.. *The Power of Platforms*. New York: The Free Press, 1997; also Whalen, endnote 1.

3. Albright, R.E. & Kappel, T.A., "Roadmapping in the corporation", *Research-Technology Management*, 46:2, March-April 2003, pp. 31-40.

4. Source: Cooper, R.G., Edgett, S.J. & Kleinschmidt, E.J., *Portfolio Management for New Products, 2ⁿᵈ edition*. Reading, MA: Perseus Book, 2002.

5. Source: Whalen, endnote 1.

6. Source of technology roadmap definition: Cooper, Edgett & Kleinschmidt, endnote 4.

7. *PDMA Handbook for New Product Development*, ed. Milton D Rosenau Jr., New York, NY: John Wiley & Sons Inc, 1996.

8. See: Meyer & Lehnerd, endnote 2.

9. Stage-Gate® is a registered trademark of the Product Development Institute Inc. This popular idea-to-launch system was developed by one of the authors. See: Cooper, R.G. *Winning at New Products: Accelerating the Process from Idea to Launch,* 3ʳᵈ edition. Reading, MA: Perseus Books, 2001.

10. A special version of Stage-Gate exists for technology developments (or science projects): see: Cooper, R.G., "Managing technology development projects – Different than traditional development projects", *Research-Technology Management*, 49;6, November-December 2006, pp. 23-31.

11. Adapted from: Phaal, R., "Roadmapping – Towards visual strategy", Proceedings, Strategic Roadmapping Conference, Heathrow, UK, 2007. Contact: University of Cambridge, Centre for Technology Management, UK.

12. Example taken from: Cate, S.N., Pilosof, D., Tait, R. & Karol, R., "The story of Clorox Green Works™ – in designing a winning green product experience Clorox cracks the code", *PDMA Visions Magazine*, XXXIII;1, March 2009, pp. 10-14.

13. An excellent outline of many superb ideation methods is found in: Cooper, R.G. & Edgett, S.J., *Generating Breakthrough New Product Ideas: Feeding the Innovation Funnel*, Product Development Institute Inc., 2007. See *www.stage-gate.com*. Our research on ideation methods and the magic quadrant diagram are found in: Cooper, R.G. & Edgett, S.J., "Ideation for product innovation: What are the best sources?", *PDMA Visions Magazine*, XXXII:1, March 2008, pp. 12-17.

14. Example take from: Beale, C.J., "How on-line communities are changing the NPD landscape – an introduction to the value of this new tool", *PDMA Visions Magazine*, XXXII:4, December 2008, pp. 14-18.

15. Source: Albright and Kappel, endnote 3.

16. For recommended sources and methods for generating breakthrough new product ideas, see: Cooper &. Edgett, endnote 13.

17. For more on scorecard evaluation methods for project selection, see Cooper, Edgett & Kleinschmidt, endnote 4; also: Cooper, R.G. & Edgett, S.J., "Ten ways to make better

portfolio and project selection decisions", *PDMA Visions Magazine*, XXX:3, June 2006, pp. 11-15.

18. A comprehensive display of possible bubble diagrams to use is in: Cooper, Edgett & Kleinschmidt, endnote 8, Chapter 1.

19. This section taken from an article by one of the authors: Cooper, R.G., "The Stage-Gate idea-to-launch process – update, what's new and NexGen systems", *Journal Product Innovation Management*, 25:3, May 2008, pp. 213-232.

20. Taken from: Garcia, M.L. & Bray, O.H., *Fundamentals of Technology Roadmapping*. Strategic Business Development Department, Sandia National Laboratories, 1997: *www.sandia.gov*

21. Taken from: Whalen, endnote 1.

22. Source: Whalen, endnote 1.

23. Source: Erler, J., "A brilliant new product idea generation program: Swarovski's i-Lab story," *Proceedings, Second International Stage-Gate Conference*, Clearwater Beach, FL, February 2008. An excellent outline of many superb ideation methods is found in: Cooper, R.G. & Edgett, S.J., *Generating Breakthrough New Product Ideas: Feeding the Innovation Funnel*, Product Development Institute Inc., 2007. Our research on ideation methods and the magic quadrant diagram are found in: Cooper, R.G. & Edgett, S.J., "Ideation for product innovation: What are the best sources?", *PDMA Visions Magazine*, XXXII:1, March 2008, pp. 12-17.

Chapter 8

1. Governance is formally defined as a set of processes, customs, policies, laws and institutions affecting the way a corporation is directed, administered or controlled. Governance also includes the relationships among the many stakeholders involved and the goals for which the corporation is governed. Adapted from Corporate Governance, Wikipedia.

2. Adapted from Kar, S., Subramanian, S., & Saran, D., "Managing global R&D operations – Lessons from the trenches", *Research-Technology Management*, 52:2 March-April 2009 pp. 14-21.

3. For more information on gatekeeping practices, see Cooper, R.G., "Effective gating: Make product innovation more productive by using gates with teeth", *Marketing Management*, March-April 2009, pp. 12-17.

4. This example has been adapted from Kirk, B., "Creating an environment for effective innovation", *Proceedings, Third International Stage-Gate Conference*, Clearwater Beach, FL, February 2009.

Made in the USA
Charleston, SC
24 November 2016